17-07-2011

Calypso's Oath

Dear Alain de Botton,

Thank you so much for your *Religie voor atheïsten*.
I would be glad if all philosophers would write as clearly as you are doing!

Kind regards

Maja P. (Wilhaam Engel)

MAJA PELLIKAAN-ENGEL

Calypso's Oath

On Biased Traditions in Philosophy

VU UNIVERSITY PRESS
AMSTERDAM

© 2010 Maja Pellikaan-Engel

All rights reserved. No part of this book may be reproduced, stored in a retrieval system, or transmitted, in any form or by any means, electronic, mechanical, photocopying, recording, or otherwise, without the prior written consent of the publisher.

First edition
Het recept van Calypso. Klassieke teksten in een hedendaags filosofisch perspectief (2004)

Translation
Margaret Kofod, Language Centre VU University

Cover illustration
Kore, c. 530–515 BC, Athens, Akropolis Museum

Cover design & typesetting
René van der Vooren, Amsterdam

VU University Press
De Boelelaan 1105
1081 HV Amsterdam
The Netherlands

info@vu-uitgeverij.nl
www.vuuitgeverij.nl

ISBN 978 90 8659 450 4 | NUR 730

Contents

1. Judging antiquity: an introduction 7
2. Calypso 15
3. Socrates and Xanthippe 28
4. Cicero 44
5. Seneca 55
6. Augustine 66
7. Fame or blame: a recapitulation 77
8. Women and the history of philosophy 81

Sources 107
Index 112
Acknowledgments 115
About the author 116

1
Judging antiquity: an introduction

Reading and making judgments

Everyone who reads selects. What takes place when we read can be compared with looking and seeing. For example, we can all watch the same film, but each of us sees the film from his or her own point of view. We focus on one picture and fail to notice another, and then we make judgments. The same thing happens with reading: even though we read the same texts, we each read the text from our own perspective and then make judgments about the contents based on our own selection of the information contained in the text — or else we simply adopt the judgment of someone in authority, without questioning it.

The same selective method of reading also plays a role in our view of literature from classical antiquity. This literature — Greek and Latin texts dating from about 800 BC to 400 AD — has left its mark on our Western civilization and is still read and studied by many, including young people at school and university. As far as the texts themselves are concerned — the actual words of the texts and their linguistic interpretation — scholars usually more or less agree. After so many centuries have passed there is of course also a certain consensus in the value judgments made on the basis of these texts. Nevertheless, in the interpretation of this information about well-known people and characters, occasionally certain elements are missed. In these cases, the interpretation of classical texts from a different point of view or on the basis of a different selection, or of a different emphasis within a selection, may well lead to different value judgments.

But not only reading is a question of selection; the same applies to writing. Writing also involves a selection process; the author writes from a particular perspective, and leaves out anything which in his or her view is not worth mentioning. For instance, things that are taken for granted are not usually stated. However, for later readers information which authors do not mention because they and their contemporary audiences would have taken it for granted may sometimes provide a vital link to understanding the text correctly. This is certainly true when an interval of a few thousand years separates text and reader. Reading is then no longer simply a question of reading what the text literally says, but also of reading what may not be said explicitly but is said implicitly, because for the author writing thousands of years ago it was the most natural thing in the world. As far as texts like these are concerned, it is very difficult to make judgments which do justice to the historic circumstances on the one hand and our contemporary norms on the other.

Classical texts in a different light

In the following chapters of this book I will examine several passages from classical antiquity. Most of these are taken from famous literary highlights of Greek and Latin literature, which will be familiar even to many readers who have not studied the classics and which are part of the standard package of classics taught at secondary schools and universities. I myself was repeatedly confronted with these texts, first at secondary school, then at university and later as a teacher of classics. Every time I read them, they always raised certain questions. I also came to realize more and more clearly that my own perception of these texts was different from the standard views and judgments that had been handed down to me. In my opinion the fact that I myself am a woman and that the standard views have usually been formed by men plays a crucial role in the differences between these views.

My point of departure in the next chapter is Homer's story about Calypso in the *Odyssey*, which dates from about 800 BC. Many readers will remember the beautiful but selfish sex bomb who kept poor Odysseus trapped on her island for years against his will and forced him to make love with her, thus being unfaithful to his wife Penelope. There he sat on the beach, the great hero, weeping with longing for his wife. But the question occurred to me: is this view that Calypso was an egoistic individual justified? It turns out that if the texts about Calypso are read from a different perspective, a totally different picture of this beautiful and sensual character emerges: that of a kind and intelligent woman, with a highly developed sense of moral values.

The following chapter is devoted to Socrates and his wife Xanthippe. Plato's *Apology*, a famous highlight of Greek literature containing an account of Socrates' defence at the trial which culminated in his death sentence in 399 BC, made a deep impression on me as a student. The *Phaedo*, which describes the last day of Socrates' life, forms as it were a sequel to the *Apology*. In the *Phaedo* we are granted a very brief glimpse of Socrates' wife Xanthippe. She was notorious for her bad temper and reputed to be an impossible woman. I wanted to understand not only Socrates but also Xanthippe and the relationship between the two. Was she really so impossible? And the philosopher himself? Does he really deserve our unquestioning admiration? My analysis of the works by Plato referred to above, supplemented by certain texts by Xenophon (like Plato a pupil of Socrates) will show that Xanthippe was actually not all that bad, whereas on closer inspection her famous husband behaved rather inconsistently and egoistically, putting her in an impossible position. Reading these widely-known texts from Greek antiquity from a different perspective thus leads to value judgments which differ from those commonly accepted: appreciation and rehabilitation for Calypso and Xanthippe, and some comments which indubitably fly in the face of the universal admiration for Socrates which often seems boundless.

A similar method is used to examine three philosophers from Roman antiquity: Cicero, from the last century before the beginning of the Common Era, Seneca from about a hundred years later and Augustine, the man who marked the end of classical antiquity and the beginning of the Christian Middle Ages around 400 AD. For the chapter on Cicero I have chosen the 'Dream of Scipio' as my point of departure. This text is the apotheosis of his famous philosophical work *De Re Publica* (The State), a work he himself regarded as his *magnum opus* and which was inspired by Plato's *State*. Stylistically the 'Dream of Scipio' is truly a masterpiece. But who, picturing the total annihilation of a city and the deportation of its people into slavery, would want to praise those responsible for these atrocities to the skies? Yet this is in fact exactly what Cicero does. Nevertheless, this philosopher is still regarded as one of the founders of Western civilization. Of course we cannot simply project our standards of judgment on people who lived two thousand years ago, but it is legitimate to express some reservations about the high esteem in which Cicero is generally held.

The passage from Tacitus' *Annals* containing his famous account of Seneca's death in 65 AD on the orders of the emperor Nero is the obvious point of departure for my discussion of Seneca. This account is very well known and can be regarded as the Roman equivalent of Socrates' last hours as described in the *Phaedo*. Seneca's death is still often put forward as the ultimate proof of his *apatheia*, the Stoic ideal of

JUDGING ANTIQUITY: AN INTRODUCTION

complete control of the emotions. But in this case we shall again see that critical reading of the text can lead to a completely different perspective.

Augustine, who is discussed in the following chapter, still wrote largely in the tradition of the classical rational philosophers. Cicero was one of the authors who played a crucial role in the development of his thinking. In turn, Augustine himself made a decisive contribution to the development of Christian thought, in particular with regard to views in the Catholic church on sexuality. I have therefore chosen a few passages about his rejection of sexuality, his repudiation of his wife, and the vision he shared with his mother. His description of this vision is particularly famous in Christian circles and is the climax of his autobiographic *Confessions*. The reader will not be surprised to find that I have unorthodox views on the famous Church Father as well.

I must stress that throughout my life it was never my aim *a priori* to criticize — quite the opposite. I was fascinated by philosophy from an early age and read everything I could get hold of on the subject. I learned that philosophers such as Socrates, Cicero, Seneca and Augustine were regarded as the great teachers of ethics and I often reflected on what they had written or what had been written about them as it was presented at school, at university or elsewhere. It was only gradually that I began to gain insight into why I did not always agree with the universally accepted views on them and questioned the glory attributed to them almost without criticism. None of them observed the two most important moral principles they might have learnt from Homer's Calypso; and not only did they themselves fail to include these principles in their theories — so did their interpreters and admirers.

However, it was not only Homer's contribution to ethics that these highly-praised philosophers overlooked. It is striking how little philosophical insight they were able to gain from their contacts with the women in their immediate vicinity. In one respect Socrates provided a splendid exception to this rule in that his so-called 'maieutic' (a word which literally means 'obstetric') method, which consisted of asking questions in order to bring forth knowledge which according to him his pupils actually already held inside them, was inspired by his mother's profession: she was a midwife. However, philosophical debate was restricted to a select group of men, who as a rule totally ignored their private lives. For them the concept of 'human being' generally refers only to men — women fall outside the picture.

At some point in their lives Socrates, Cicero, Seneca and Augustine all sent their wives away — albeit in completely different circumstances and in completely different ways — as though they were insignificant extras in their own much more important lives as philosophers. In contrast to their undervaluation of their spouses, in some cases the same philosophers attached exaggerated importance to certain other women in their lives: Cicero adored his daughter Tullia, Augustine his mother Monica. However, this overvaluation failed to lead to more balanced views in their philosophical discussions of man and society. As a result of the imbalance in Cicero's and Augustine's private relationships, both of them eventually took the view that it is better for a philosopher not to marry.

The conclusion seems inevitable that the personal incapacity of the famous philosophers discussed in this book — their incapacity to integrate women into their lives and work as equal human beings — played an important role in creating an imbalance in the history of philosophical thought, in which women are no more than forgotten minor players.

JUDGING ANTIQUITY: AN INTRODUCTION

Philosophical perspective

The last chapter discusses the question of who has made the value judgments on these texts from classical antiquity —judgments which are now commonly accepted. Because these are texts by philosophers or at least texts with philosophical implications, and because the value judgments on them have been passed down mainly in the context of academic philosophy, any criticism of these texts leads almost automatically to criticism of the prevailing point of view in academic philosophy. A short outline of two and a half thousand years of history of philosophy, which goes against the grain by presenting only the names and works of almost forgotten women philosophers, will illustrate the one-sidedness of the various perspectives from which the classical texts have usually been read and judged — a one-sidedness which can be attributed to the fact that to date men have had a virtually absolute monopoly on the formation of these judgments. This is a monopoly which, in spite of several waves of feminism, has even today not received sufficient scrutiny. As a result, it seems as though the commonly accepted judgments represent a completed process. However, in my opinion the evaluation of classical texts is an unfinished process and some commonly accepted interpretations are in urgent need of reconsideration.

The re-evaluation of certain value judgments which seem to be have been firmly established for centuries is not purely an academic question. Since these judgments relate to figures who still play an important role in our cultural life and still feature in the curriculum for many young people at school or university so that they are brought to life practically every day, it is important that people should become aware of the selective nature of the traditional views and learn to question the old texts and look at them in a new light. It does not really even matter whether the evaluations are of characters from literature, such as Calypso, or historical individuals from a more or less distant past, or contemporary figures. The perspective from which judgments are made is directly related to the formation of one's own personal views and attitude to life. This is why it is important when making judgments to weigh all the aspects against each other and to identify any blind spots there may be in commonly accepted views. Surely none of us wants to suffer from blind spots, let alone pass them on to succeeding generations at our schools and universities.

2
Calypso

Double standard

It is not generally known, but the first feminist speech in Western civilization is to be found in Homer's *Odyssey*. Homer's epics, the *Iliad* and the *Odyssey*, are the oldest works of Greek literature, dating from about 800 BC. The *Odyssey* is the story of Odysseus, who is away from his home for ten years fighting in the Trojan war, and then takes another ten years to get back to his wife Penelope. During his voyage home he has all sorts of adventures. At a certain point, after he has been living with the goddess Calypso for seven years, the gods decide that she must send him home. Zeus sends Hermes, messenger of the gods, to inform her of this command. Her reaction is furious:

> Cruel are you, you gods, and quick to envy above all others, seeing that you begrudge goddesses that they should mate with men openly, if any takes a mortal as her own bedfellow. Thus, when rosy-fingered Dawn took to herself Orion, you gods that live at ease begrudged her, till in Ortygia chaste Artemis of the golden throne assailed him with her gentle shafts and slew him. Thus too, when fair-tressed Demeter, yielding to her passion, lay in love with Iasion in the thrice-plowed fallow land, Zeus was not long without knowledge of it, but smote him with his bright thunderbolt and slew him. And in this way again do you now begrudge me, you gods, that a mortal man should become my companion. Him I

saved when he was bestriding the keel and all alone, for Zeus had struck his swift ship with his bright thunderbolt and had shattered it in the midst of the wine-dark sea. There all the rest of his noble comrades perished, but as for him, the wind and the waves, as they bore him, brought him here. Him I welcomed kindly and gave him food, and said that I would make him immortal and ageless all his days. (*Od.* 5. 118-136, tr. A. T. Murray, revised by George E. Dimock, Loeb Classical Library.)

Calypso's reaction is emotional; but at the same time her arguments are rational and include a point of criticism which is astonishing for the time. She attacks the double standard which did not allow female gods to enjoy open relations with mortal men, while relations of the same kind between male gods and mortal women were widely known and generally accepted. She does not need to give examples.

Secondly, she argues that Zeus in particular is hardly entitled to speak, in view of his treatment of Odysseus' interests seven years previously; he had had him shipwrecked on the high seas so that he was almost killed. She had rescued him and they had come to be lovers; but now Zeus was ordering her to send Odysseus home.

Then Calypso says that she had wanted to give Odysseus immortality and ageless youth. This implies that she, an unmarried goddess, had hoped for a permanent bond. In other words, her intentions in her relationship with Odysseus were very serious, whereas everyone knew that the amorous adventures of Zeus, ruler of the gods and adulterer, were much less serious.

Calypso's oath

In spite of these arguments, Calypso decides to let Odysseus go. Zeus's command was a pivotal factor in a difficult decision she has had to make for herself. She has been in an ambivalent position; she still loves Odysseus, but clearly his love for her has all but vanished: the only thing he wants is to go home. Evidently Calypso has been thinking about a solution for this dilemma for quite some time; when she tells Odysseus about her decision, she has already thought out a complete course of action. She suggests that he should build a ship to set out on the long voyage home; she herself will provide him with everything he needs to do so.

At first Odysseus does not trust her and asks her to swear a solemn oath as proof of the sincerity of her intentions. The fact that the crafty Odysseus is not inclined to trust her makes her laugh, but she agrees to his request immediately and calls on heaven and earth and the underworld as well to bear witness. Having reassured him, she concludes her oath as follows:

> But I am only thinking of and shall ponder on what
> I should devise for myself, if I were in your straits;
> for my mind is righteous and the heart in this breast
> of mine is not of iron, but has compassion.
> (*Od.* 5. 188-91, tr. M. Pellikaan-Engel.)

The simplicity of this utterance reminds one of a home recipe rather than the declaration of a fundamental moral principle. And as a rule no more is seen in it than a personal statement which fits the context. But the fact that she says '*for* my mind is righteous' shows that she regards it as a basic moral obligation to put oneself in the position of the other person who is in a difficult situation and with that position as a point of departure to use one's intelligence to devise a solution. The fact that she refers to the use of her mind with three different verbs to (I am thinking of, I shall ponder, I should devise) suggests both the intensity and duration of her thought process and the diversity of the options she has considered. And this empathy — putting oneself in the position of another — does not come forth from a 'heart of iron', armoured against feelings, but a heart that 'has compassion', which knows its own feelings and is therefore capable of imagining someone else's.

In this passage, from the oldest text of Western literature, we find this moral principle: put yourself in the position of the other, imagine the feelings that person has in that situation, and then treat that person as you would want to be treated if you were in that situation. And it is explicitly the activity of both mind *and* heart, reason combined with empathy, which for Calypso is the key to morally right actions. Empathy as an indispensable ingredient of morality: from our perspective it seems obvious, but in the Greek patriarchal class society of around 800 BC it was certainly not something that was taken for granted. This moral position, which is anything but self-centred, elitist or noncommittal, is what Homer has Calypso express: Calypso, who is so often seen as the egoistic, oversexed goddess who kept the poor, faithful mortal Odysseus trapped on her island for seven years against his will.

For this is more or less the description many people will remember from the beginning of the Odyssey, when the goddess Athena begs her father Zeus to free Odysseus from the power of Calypso, 'daughter of the malevolent Atlas':

> His daughter it is that keeps back that unfortunate, sorrowing man; and continually with soft and wheedling words she beguiles him that he may forget Ithaca. But

Odysseus, in his longing to see were it but the smoke leaping up from his own land, yearns to die. (*Od.* 1.55-59, tr. A. T. Murray, revised by George E. Dimock, Loeb Classical Library.)

The picture of Calypso given here by the goddess Athena is certainly not very flattering. The phrase 'daughter of the malevolent Atlas' implies that Calypso herself is likely to be malevolent as well; her constant attempts to seduce Odysseus evoke a picture of nauseating sexual importunity; the fact that she is keeping him trapped on her island against his will can certainly be regarded as proof of her egoism. This is the first impression Homer's readers are given of Calypso — and first impressions are important!

But anyone who concludes that Calypso was a malicious, egoistic nymphomaniac is forgetting who it was who gave this description: the goddess Athena, herself uninterested in sex and obviously angered by the sensual Calypso's sexual advances towards Odysseus, Athena's own favourite. The conclusion would also leave the previous relationship between Calypso and Odysseus out of the equation — a relationship which had lasted seven years. At the point when the story begins, the goddess *no longer* pleased him (*Od.* 5.153). Apparently she originally had, and during those seven years Odysseus must have proved himself a convincing lover; otherwise it would be difficult to explain Calypso's fury at the fact that she has to send her lover away. However, by this time things have changed: he spends his days weeping on the beach, longing for his home and his wife Penelope, but still sleeps with the goddess at night — although under duress, the text tells us. What the nature of this duress might have been is not clear. It is in fact difficult to imagine how anyone could force someone to make love in such a way as to satisfy both parties. Apparently the only factors causing Odysseus' ambivalent attitude are the practical situation — he finds himself on a remote island and there is no ship available — and his own susceptibility to the charms of Calypso's beauty and love. Even in the night after she has told him of her decision, again they *both* enjoy love, remaining by each other's side (*Od.* 5.227). This is the conclusion of a serious love affair. Ultimately Odysseus chooses Penelope over Calypso.

Though her heart is bleeding, the goddess respects his choice and puts the principle she has expressed into action. Resolutely and with technical expertise she shows Odysseus where to find the materials to build his ship, provides him with the tools he needs and brings him cloth for the sail. She herself stocks the ship with plenty of appetizing provisions and skins of water and wine; she bathes him, gives him clean clothing and ensures a favourable wind. With a happy heart he spreads his sail and off he goes — home to Penelope. There is no mention of a farewell; it is as though that is simply too much to expect from him.

Marital fidelity

Homer's work can be read as one long plea for marital fidelity. In the *Iliad* he depicts the disastrous consequences of the infidelity of the beautiful Helen: the bloody war at Troy which lasted ten years. The essence of the *Odyssey* is the story of how difficult it is to achieve lifelong marital fidelity. Penelope succeeds in remaining completely faithful to her husband, even when he has been missing for years and a large group of men are trying to frustrate her fidelity. Odysseus is less single-minded. It takes him ten years to return from Troy. He spends one whole year with the goddess Circe, even though there does not seem to be any need for this. Only when his men start to complain does he decide to press on. He stays with Calypso for seven years.

He thus spends a total of eight of those ten years with the two goddesses, enjoying their loving embraces before he shakes off his ambivalence and attempts to sail straight back to Penelope.

We must bear in mind that at that time a double standard in marital relationships was universally accepted. Women had to be faithful to their husbands; men were entitled to be unfaithful. Men usually practised this right on their female slaves, who were also supposed to be completely faithful to their masters. If they were not, they were severely punished. For example, when he returned to Ithaca Odysseus himself resolutely ordered the female slaves who had consorted — of their own free will or not — with Penelope's suitors to be killed, 'with long, pointed swords'. Homer then describes how Odysseus' son carried out this order, but swore that he would give them only the less honourable death of hanging. He stretched out a hawser and pulled it tight, high enough that none of the women would touch the ground:

> And as when long-winged thrushes or doves fall into a snare that is set in a thicket, as they seek to reach their resting-place, and hateful is the bed that gives them welcome, even so the women held their heads in a row, and round the necks of all nooses were laid, that they might die most piteously. And they writhed a little while with their feet, but not long. (*Od.* 22.468-473, tr. A.T. Murray, revised by George E. Dimock, Loeb Classical Library.)

Homer ends his account of the women's execution with this gripping simile, which is not a neutral description. The image chosen, of innocent birds like thrushes or doves dying such a horrible death, does not only suggest pity for the victims. The blind bard also seems to want to exonerate them and therefore to silently criticize the judgment of

Odysseus, the man who had himself been unfaithful for so long.

This veiled criticism is in keeping with the views expressed by Calypso about the double standard: that it is unjust that different standards apply to male gods than to female gods. This account of the murder of the female slaves contains a certain criticism of the double moral standard on which the death sentence was based. Homer seems to be implying that he thinks it is equally unjust that among mortals men are judged according to different standards than women.

It is surprising that this basic theme in Homer, marital fidelity, is so seldom discussed. Many people remember Odysseus' numerous adventures, and Penelope's fidelity has always made a great impression. Usually Odysseus' infidelity is ignored; and the fact that almost three thousand years ago Homer apparently wanted to criticize the unfairness of the assymetrical role patterns attributed to men and women is almost entirely overlooked; nevertheless, this is the most obvious interpretation of the angry outburst about the double standard which he puts into Calypso's mouth.

Homer as a source of ethics

As we have seen, Homer has Calypso express two progressive ideas: criticism of the double standard, and the principle of treating another as you would want to be treated yourself in the same situation. These ideas sprang from a moral position which was extremely progressive for the time, assuming as it did that status and gender — she was goddess, he a mortal man — made no difference. Why then have these radical ethical views received so little attention?

One important reason must be the fact that views like these were unwelcome in the patriarchal society of antiquity — and they remained unwelcome for centuries. Nobody likes to renounce privileges. If people challenge them, the best response is not to take these people seriously. This is where the problem lies: for Homer himself was and is certainly regarded as an authority, but he put these progressive ideas in the mouth of his character Calypso, who can easily be reduced to the caricature of an oversexed goddess who forced the poor hero Odysseus to sleep with her. Obviously there is no need to take any notice of what someone like this says.

Another reason must be the way she presented her message. When she attacked the double standard she was angry and therefore clearly emotional, and what someone says in an emotional outburst is usually not taken very seriously. Emotionality and rationality are often seen as mutually exclusive. However, in Calypso Homer presents a mindset in which emotions and rationality complement each other: her arguments were rational, and she was justified in being angry about the double standard manifested in the interference of her fellow gods.

Homer's formulation of the basic principles of moral behaviour is of a staggering simplicity. He has Calypso say what she regards as morally right in a very down-to-earth way, in a statement in the first person about her personal approach, not in the form of an authoritarian imperative as to how people should behave in general — she is not laying down the law for anyone — but very simply:

> I am only thinking of and shall ponder on what I should devise for myself, if I were in your straits.

However, the self-assured addition 'for my mind is righteous' does imply that she regards her words as universally valid. 'I act in this way because my mind is righteous' implies that people whose minds are righteous act in this way. The fact that this is the final sentence of a solemn oath indicates that the attitude she expresses is meant very seriously.

Here it is as though Homer is leading us to the very source of ethics. But just as it is easy to miss the source of a river when you are walking through the countryside because it may be very inconspicuous — if you do notice it and realize how big the stream is a little further down you may be quite surprised — in the same way the implications of these simple words spoken by Calypso have usually been overlooked in the history of ethics. But however simply formulated, the words Homer has placed in the mouth of his fictional character Calypso express the most essential basic principle of human ethics. Then, in the next passage, which is equally impressive and just as light in tone, the poet shows us how the goddess puts her own principle of behaviour into practice. She herself brings the cloth for the sails and provisions on board so that the man she loves can leave her. It is an excellent example of the generosity of heart the moral law sometimes demands of us.

Basically Calypso's principle encapsulates the same moral message as that of the later *New Testament:*

> And as you wish that men would do to you, do so to them. (Luke 6.31.)

Readers schooled in philosophy may be more inclined to think of the categorical imperative postulated by Kant, the famous eighteenth-century philosopher:

> Act as if the maxim from which you act were to become through your will a universal law.

This is a precise academic formulation: authoritative, in the imperative, detached. The readers have to climb up to Kant's level of abstraction — if they want to and if they are able to; for the somewhat laborious wording of Kant's moral guideline is rather difficult to fix in one's mind and to capture in one's heart. We shall also see that Kant himself did not always think through all the consequences of his own maxims.

Archetype/prototype

No matter what sensible things the goddess Calypso may have said, most people are still more likely to see her as the beautiful and seductive woman to whom the faithful hero Odysseus fell victim. It seems that Calypso herself has fallen victim to a reduction of her character — the same sort of reduction often applied to her Olympian fellow goddesses, namely a reduction from individual to archetype. The goddess Athena (Minerva to the Romans) is usually reduced to an asexual intellectual, Aphrodite (Venus) to a frivolous sex object and Hera (Juno) to a respectable but rather boring wife-mother. According to the American classics scholar Sarah Pomeroy modern women still suffer today from these caricatural archetypes. It is as though women in particular must always be categorized according to one of these archetypes, while in truth all human beings have aspects of every type within them.

This is exactly what happened with Calypso. Her sensuality is always overemphasized, though she is also represented by Homer as an intelligent woman with a highly developed moral sense, who proved with her touching solicitude for Odysseus that her moral position, based on empathy, was not just empty words.

However, this reductionist 'sex bomb' image is not the only image of Calypso which has arisen: she has also become the literary prototype of the woman who begins a sincere love relationship with a man who has a different agenda and will therefore eventually leave her. This is a frequently recurring theme in literature. I will limit myself here to two examples of authors for whom Homer's Calypso was a source of inspiration.

The first is the Roman poet Virgil who, about eight centuries after Homer, modelled his *Aeneid* on Homer's work, in a completely original way. In this epic Virgil sublimely recreates the image of Calypso in the character of Dido, queen of Carthage, a young city on the coast of Africa. When the hero Aeneas is washed up there by a storm he is hospitably received by the beautiful Dido. Soon they are passionately in love; heaven and earth bear witness to their first lovemaking. Dido expects Aeneas to stay with her and govern Carthage by her side, but the 'dutiful' (*pius*) Aeneas knows his destiny: he must go to Italy, where, as father of the nation and a model of virtue, he is to lay the foundations of the great Roman Empire. After an inner struggle he sails away, like a thief in the night. Dido commits suicide... Sometimes we can still hear her immortal voice in Purcell's beautiful opera *Dido and Aeneas* or Berlioz's *Les Troyens*.

My second example is from contemporary literature: the novel *L'Ignorance* by the Czech author Milan Kundera who now lives in France. The impossible situation of the emigrant, who is no longer at home anywhere and can no longer find enduring love anywhere, is an important theme in this book. In the following quotation taken from the English translation of the novel, we are reminded of Calypso:

> Calypso, ah, Calypso! I often think about her. She loved Odysseus. They lived together for seven years. We do not know how long Odysseus shared Penelope's bed, but certainly not so long as that. And yet we extol Penelope's pain and sneer at Calypso's tears. (*Ignorance* p. 9, tr. Linda Asher.)

Kundera's plea for compassion with Calypso is certainly

justified. However, this should not detract from our compassion with Penelope, who remained faithful to her missing husband. Both women are presented by Homer as strong and admirable moral characters.

Homer's creation Calypso, the goddess who lived far away from her Olympian fellow gods on a secluded island, can also be seen as the literary prototype of a talented woman philosopher. Her insight that double standards are morally unacceptable and that both empathy and intelligence are basic ingredients of morally responsible behaviour is in fact part of the foundations of ethics. But it is not only Homer's character Calypso who never made it into the philosophy textbooks; a whole series of later women philosophers, whose historical existence cannot be denied and who in some cases formulated surprising insights, are usually also ignored in these textbooks. I will come back to this point in a later chapter.

3
Socrates and Xanthippe

Shrew

'Xanthippe was a shrew'. When I was a little girl I had to copy the Dutch equivalent of this sentence in my exercise book to practise the capital X. I can still remember the little scene that took place when I asked the teacher who Xanthippe was and she told me it wasn't important. Since I thought I should not be made to write down a sentence I did not understand, an atmosphere of tension arose in the class. By now the other children had already filled in half a page — but my page was still empty. I never received an answer to my question and eventually of course I had to give in. Many generations must have been indoctrinated by this statement about Xanthippe.

But who was Xanthippe? She was the wife of Socrates, the famous Athenian philosopher who lived from 469 to 399 BC. We know quite a lot about him through his pupils Plato and Xenophon, but fortunately also a little about her. And what we do know about her seems to be no more than a confirmation of the sentence I had to practise writing. In Xenophon's *Symposium* we read a contemporary's description of her:

> the most ill-tempered of all women of the present, the past and probably also the future. (*Symp.* II.10.)

You might ask yourself why Socrates had married her then. So did his friends. In the same passage of the *Symposium*

Xenophon, who had rather a practical mindset, gives us one reason supplied by Socrates himself. Xenophon tells us about a dancing girl who has given an extremely skilful performance while Socrates and his companions are drinking. Socrates says that she has provided one of many proofs that women are in no way inferior to men except in physical strength; and that everyone present should feel confident of being able to teach his wife any skill he wants to. Surprised, his friend Antisthenes responds by asking him why then he does not train Xanthippe himself, ending his question with the description quoted above.

In his answer Socrates makes use of a simile which alludes to the literal meaning of his wife's name: blond mare. He says that men who want to become expert horsemen do not buy tame horses but high-spirited ones, because if they can control them they can easily control other horses.

> And it is the same with me; I took her because I wish to deal and associate with human beings in general and was quite sure that if I could tolerate her, I could easily cope with the rest of mankind. (*Symp.* II,10.)

Poor Xanthippe — chosen because she was challenging material to practise on! In the textbook I used as a teacher at school the only comment made on this argument put forward by Socrates was that he had put a 'fine twist' on his relationship with Xanthippe. The textbook might at least have added that today Socrates' behaviour should be denounced on moral grounds, for example with reference to Kant's maxim that a human being may never be used only as a means for one's own purposes.

The view expressed by Socrates that women are in no way inferior to men seems progressive, but — contrary to what one might expect — in the rest of this passage he expresses views which are completely in keeping with the social relationships of his time: men were capable of action, they 'took' wives, whom they could then tutor and teach skills as they saw fit. Women were the property first of their fathers and then of their husbands, and had no rights of their own, even in the so-called progressive and democratic state of Athens at that time. With few exceptions, girls and women were not educated. They were just supposed to stay at home and fulfil their duties.

Apparently Xanthippe had expected more from her life and had expressed this with some anger and frustration. However, Socrates had not chosen her to make her life more tolerable, but to practise his own tolerance in order to improve his own social life. Socrates is regarded as the founder of ethics. He is famous for his rationalistic view of virtue: anyone who knows what is right will act in accordance with that knowledge. We shall examine whether he tried to apply this insight with respect to his own marriage and family and whether he thought with any empathy — according to Calypso's recipe — about the possibility of improving Xanthippe's lot and her temper.

Good mother

In another text by Xenophon Socrates indicates a second reason for choosing Xanthippe as his wife. In his *Memorabilia* Xenophon gives an account of a conversation between Socrates and his eldest son, who had complained about an angry outburst by his mother. Socrates rebukes him and tells him he should be grateful to his mother, because she had given birth to him and brought him up. Here he also gives a rational explanation of his choice of Xanthippe and goes on to discuss the roles of husband and wife in marriage. Here is a passage from his words to his son:

> Surely you don't think human beings produce children for the sake of lust, when the streets and brothels are

full of means to satisfy that? Obviously we select as wives those women who would bear us the best children, and then marry them and have children with them. The man supports the woman who will have children with him and provides the future children with whatever he thinks will benefit them in life, in as large a quantity as he can. The woman, having conceived, bears this heavy burden of pregnancy, risking her life, and sharing her own food with her child; and when with much labour she has endured to the end and given birth, she feeds it and cares for it, although she has not yet received any benefits from this, and the baby does not know who is treating it so well and is not even able to make its wants known; but guessing what is good for it and what it likes, she tries to supply these things, and she feeds it for a long time, and endures toil day and night, not knowing what thanks she will get. (*Mem.* II.II.4-6.)

This passage suggests that Socrates himself had selected Xanthippe very deliberately as the most suitable future mother of his children and that he had an eye for what a mother does — her capacity to empathize with her babies and to meet their needs. Apparently Xanthippe also fits into this picture of a loving mother which he presents to his son. This certainly places her in a much more favourable light than the description we saw before of Xanthippe as the most ill-tempered woman of all times!

We also see something else: in the first sentence Socrates speaks of 'human beings' — but then it immediately becomes clear that he is referring only to free, adult men. The use of terms like this which seem to be generic but actually have a veiled sex-specific meaning will be exposed several times in this book.

Paternal duties

As we have seen, according to Socrates it was a man's duty to support his wife and provide his children with everything he thought they needed, in as great a quantity as possible. It will be interesting to see how Socrates discharged the paternal duties he described. To do this, we will conduct a brief reconstruction.

Socrates was sentenced to death in 399 BC — I will come back to this in more detail at a later point — when he was 70 years old. In his defence at the trial, as recorded by Plato in the *Apology*, he says that after a statement by the Delphic oracle he felt called to devote the rest of his life to philosophy. He says repeatedly that as a result of his calling to philosophy he has had no time to earn money or to take care of his family and that he has lived in poverty. We do not know exactly when this calling became apparent to him, but in the play *The Clouds* dating from 423 Aristophanes pokes fun at Socrates as a full-time philosopher. The calling must therefore have dated from considerably earlier than 423, in other words well before Socrates turned forty-six. In the *Apology* Socrates says that at present — i.e. when he is seventy — he has three sons; the eldest is an adolescent, probably about fifteen, the other two still quite young. This means that he must have had the eldest when he was over fifty, and the two youngest when he was well into his sixties.

This arithmetic makes it clear that *after* his calling, which he considered incompatible with something so banal as earning money, Socrates deliberately fathered children, but failed to fulfil the duty of care he himself described. This suggests that far from improving Xanthippe's lot, in line with Calypso's carefully considered principle of empathy, Socrates made things worse for her. The cupboards in Socrates' little house must have been very bare and it must have been almost impossible for Xanthippe to bring up their children.

She was probably very energetic and resourceful. It was in fact she who paid the price for his calling.

Fulltime philosopher

For Socrates himself his calling was apparently not a heavy burden. At least, he claims that

> to talk every day about virtue and the other things about which you hear me talking and examining myself and others is the greatest good to man, and that the unexamined life is not worth living. (*Apol.* 38a, tr. H.N. Fowler.)

The term 'man' used in the generic sense seems to give his claim a universal validity, suggesting that it applies to 'the human species'. It sounds impressive; but really he can only have meant 'people like us'. Xanthippe, other members of her sex and slaves were not included. They just had to get on with their daily work.

Concepts such as virtue and justice were standard themes for Socrates. He discussed them every day on the streets and at the marketplace with all and sundry. In his dialogues — which have come to be known as Socratic dialogues — he constantly subjected other people's opinions to critical analysis. But his partners in these dialogues were exclusively men. Of course he could also have had conversations like these with his own wife at home. Perhaps the two of them could have analysed together and come to the conclusion that there were in fact rational grounds for her notorious fits of bad temper and that she was justified in complaining that he only *talked* about virtue and justice, whereas she herself constantly had to *do* what she regarded as virtuous and just.

Trial and condemnation

In practically all philosophy textbooks Socrates is still presented as the great model of a philosopher whose life and doctrine were one. And on certain occasions he proved convincingly that he was prepared to do what was right even in the face of death, for example when he rescued his friend Alcibiades on the battlefield. However, it was his attitude during the trial culminating in his death sentence and the way he bore his lot that are regarded as the ultimate proof.

Perhaps it will be helpful to provide a little background information in relation to Socrates' trial — the trial which brought him eternal glory. Athens was a democracy in the sense that all free, male, adult native Athenians had the right to vote as citizens of Athens and that they took turns in being responsible for administrative tasks and jury duties. In this democratic state Socrates was charged in 399 BC on two counts: impiety, i.e. that he had failed to venerate the state gods, and corrupting the youth, i.e. that he had exercised a bad influence on young people. In the textbooks these charges are usually brushed aside as being completely ungrounded, and in fact they can only be comprehended against the background of the political situation in which Athens found itself at that time. Various studies have been devoted to this context, such as the interesting book *The Trial of Socrates* by the American journalist Izzy F. Stone. Below I will give a very brief summary of the events surrounding the trial and people involved. Similar outlines are to be found in many concise history books.

In 404 BC the Athenians, who had enjoyed hegemony at sea for many years, suffered a crushing defeat at the hands of the Spartans after the dramatic Peloponnesian war, which had begun in 431 and during the course of which the male population of Athens had been decimated. The Athenians had been forced to hand over their fleet and to demolish the protective walls between the city of Athens and the harbour of Piraeus.

Various friends and pupils of Socrates played a rather dubious role in this story, especially Alcibiades, a good friend of Socrates. Accusations made against him of blasphemy (he was said to have ridiculed the sacred mysteries of Eleusis when he was drunk and one night to have knocked off the heads of the statues of Hermes which stood on squares and crossings in Athens) were probably true. Even in times of peace excesses like this were held to be subversive, let alone in a situation of war. It is certain that in 415 Alcibiades led a risky military expedition to Sicily which ended fatally for thousands of Athenians and their allies. However, when he was called back to Athens on account of an official charge of blasphemy, he defected to the Spartans and advised them to blockade the Athenians' supply of food and the line of communication with their silver mines. This advice must certainly have contributed to the eventual defeat of Athens. The opportunist Alcibiades did not remain loyal to the Spartans either, and this proved fatal to him: in 404 he was murdered on the orders of a Spartan general.

Let us return to the charge against Socrates. There is no evidence to suggest anything reprehensible in Socrates' own attitude in this war, and of course he cannot be blamed for the undemocratic sympathies of several of his friends and ex-pupils or for Alcibiades' impiety and offensive behaviour. On the other hand, Alcibiades had been a close younger friend of Socrates — in Plato's *Symposium* Alcibiades himself speaks quite openly about the erotic aspects of Socrates' friendships — and the jury would certainly have been aware of this. Apparently Socrates had not had a very positive influence on Alcibiades, in spite of being on such intimate terms with him, and the jury may well have seen this as the equivalent of having a negative influence. The same would have applied, though to a lesser extent, to his relationships with a number of other younger men. Seen against the dramatic background of the social turmoil in Athens at the time it is not entirely incomprehensible that Socrates was accused of impiety and corrupting the young.

Socrates then delivered a speech in his defence, of which Plato left us an impressive account in his *Apology*. In this defence Socrates refers to his divine calling to the life of a philosopher. The jury, consisting of five hundred men, retired to consider their verdict, and at the first vote Socrates was found guilty by a small majority. The penalty was death. According to the procedural rules he then had the option of suggesting a different penalty: exile or a fine, for example. Socrates remained certain of his innocence:

> I am convinced that I have never intentionally wronged anyone. (*Apol.* 37A.)

And precisely because he is so convinced that he has never wronged anyone else, he declares that he does not want to wrong himself either. In fact, he says, he really deserves remuneration rather than punishment. His reasoning goes like this: by my life as a philosopher I have served the state every day, and therefore I am entitled to the dinner given free of charge to men of merit. (These meals were provided daily at the Prytaneion, the Athenian 'town hall'.) But even Socrates realized that claiming an honour as a punishment might seem a little too arrogant, and eventually he offered to pay a fine: thirty minae, a modest sum for which his friends would be sureties. With this attitude Socrates lost more of the jury's sympathy and his trial culminated in a definite death sentence in the next round of votes — with a clear majority in favour.

Blind spot

Of course in our eyes Socrates' death sentence cannot be justified. But was it true that he had never wronged anyone? Earlier in this chapter we saw that he told his son it was a man's duty to support his wife and family. In the *Apology* he says that because of his calling he has had no time to earn money and take care of his family, and that he has lived in great poverty. Actually, thanks to his work he often enjoyed free dinners at the homes of his rich friends. It was his wife and children who suffered on account of his calling. Although in his own perception Socrates never wronged anyone, in my opinion this was a blind spot in his self-image.

However, Socrates himself even claims a sort of divine sanction for his conduct. He sometimes refers to his *daimonion* — his inner voice — which in his own words (*Apol.* 40A) was constantly in the habit of opposing him if he was going to do something wrong, even if it was only a trifling matter. By using this word *daimonion*, which literally refers to a divine manifestation, he attributes a divine aura to this inner voice, which therefore compels respect. Perhaps the divine voice might have been a little more critical when Socrates was considering marrying Xanthippe and having children with her. In the lecture he gives his son on the tasks and duties of marriage he says that his marriage to Xanthippe was the result of a conscious decision. And he fathered his children *after* his calling had been manifested to him. But if he really believed that his calling was incompatible with the duty to care for a family and the lowly business of earning money, and if he nevertheless wanted to follow this calling, then surely the *daimonion* — his critical inner voice — should have made itself heard with respect to these important decisions and Socrates should not have started a family at all.

Whichever way you look at it — as a blind spot in Socrates' perception of himself or a blind spot on the part of his *daimonion* —, criticism of Socrates on this score is surely justified, even though it seems almost like a form of sacrilege. Practically all the textbooks completely agree with Plato's opinion that Socrates was 'the best and wisest and most righteous man' (*Phaedo* 118). However, in my opinion it is also a blind spot in the textbooks that these points of criticism have scarcely ever been discussed.

Different times

Perhaps you might think that such criticism is inappropriate because ideas like this were simply not discussed in philosophic circles in Athens around 400 BC. But the interesting thing is that in fact they were! Plato tells us that when Socrates was already in prison his friend Crito tried to persuade him to run away to Thessaly. With some financial assistance and some good friends there it was definitely an option, and Crito was keen to arrange it. One of his arguments was that surely Socrates could not leave his children behind as orphans:

> Either one ought not to beget children, or one ought to stay by them and bring them up and educate them. (*Crito* 45D, tr. H. N. Fowler.)

said Crito, according to Plato. In his answer Socrates does in fact go into this subject:

> But the considerations you suggest, about [...] bringing up my children, these are really, Crito, the reflections of those who lightly put men to death, and would bring them to life again, if they could, without sense, I mean

the multitude. But *we* must consider... (*Crito* 48C, tr. H. N. Fowler.)

Here Socrates is implying that those who sentenced him to death were in the habit of taking decisions about life and death too lightly, without sound reasons. And with his emphatic 'but *we*' he distances himself from them, claiming that unlike them he himself bases decisions of this kind on rational principles. However, one might wonder if it was such a rational decision to deliberately father children at an advanced age, after his calling had already manifested itself, since in connection with that calling he was unable or unwilling to take responsibility for the care of his family. He did not kill rashly, but he fathered children rashly. One cannot help wondering whether there is really so much difference with regard to assuming responsibility for decisions relating to putting people to death and calling them to life.

It is striking that Plato pays so much attention here to paternal responsibility. Perhaps it is an indication of Plato's own reasons for not marrying and not having children. The reason is usually thought to be his homosexuality; but in Athens at that time homosexuality was no reason not to marry. Many men led active homosexual lives and then married a much younger woman at a later age, specifically in order to have children. This was also the case with Socrates. The question of whether or not to marry and father children was one familiar to men of that time. Women, on the other hand, had no right to self-determination whatsoever — and therefore no say in matters of pregnancy either. We read nothing about this: what is taken for granted is not mentioned.

Last day

In the *Phaedo* Plato gives a detailed account of the last day of Socrates' life. Plato tells us that he himself was unable to be there because he was ill, and that his description is based on what he has heard from the young Phaedo, who had seen everything as an eye witness.

Xanthippe had spent the last night with her husband in the prison, along with their youngest child. Early in the morning Socrates' friends were allowed to enter — more than fifteen of them. Phaedo says:

> We went in then and found Socrates just released from his fetters and Xanthippe — you know her — with his little son in her arms, sitting beside him. Now when Xanthippe saw us, she cried out and said the kind of thing that women always do say: 'Oh Socrates, this is the last time now that your friends will speak to you or you to them.' And Socrates glanced at Crito and said, 'Crito, let somebody take her home.' And some of Crito's people took her away wailing and beating her breast. (*Phaedo* 60A, tr. H. N. Fowler.)

The condescending way Phaedo talks about Xanthippe here ('she said the kind of thing that women always do say') shows little respect on his part for Socrates' partner in marriage and for women in general. But when he refers to their youngest child, whom she was probably still breast-feeding, as 'his little son', he leaves her out of the picture altogether.

In the meantime it is clear that Xanthippe herself tried to communicate with her husband right to the last minute. Just one sentence of what she ever said has been passed down to us in direct speech:

> Oh Socrates, this is the last time now that your friends will speak to you or you to them.

Obviously she is trying to put herself in Socrates' position: a man in prison, who is to be executed that same day and will now talk to his friends for the very last time. Clearly she is aware of this and is trying to gauge how he feels: in other words, she shows empathy.

But Socrates does not even look at his wife, the course of whose life has been so fundamentally determined by his actions. Glancing at his friend, he says:

> Crito, let somebody take her home.

Not only Phaedo, but Socrates himself talks about Xanthippe only in the third person: she is present but excluded. His friends are more important to him and he sends her away without paying any further attention to her.

Off she goes, distressed and distraught — excluded, and condemned to the fate of a widow who will have to manage on her own with her small children. The whole tragedy of her marriage is encapsulated in this passage. In his book *Die grossen Philosophen* (p. 118) Karl Jaspers interprets this harrowing scene, which contains not a single word or gesture of leavetaking, as 'a friendly farewell'. Evidently there are different ways of looking at it.

Socrates goes on talking to his friends quite happily — unmoved by the fate awaiting his wife and children. And just as unmoved by the fate of death which awaits himself. Even in these circumstances he gives a wonderful example of his '*ataraxia*', his famous imperturbability. And soon his words take off again on the wings of philosophy.

During the afternoon he withdraws into the bathroom with Crito to wash so that the women will not be burdened with washing his corpse. Plato says that then, in the presence of Crito, he also meets his three children and the women of his family. Presumably Xanthippe was there as well, but the text gives us no further information on this point.

Then Socrates returns to his friends. He continues to talk to them for a while, in good spirits, and then he drinks the poisoned cup. His friends burst into tears. Socrates calms them with a reprimand. Then he dies, serene and controlled, after speaking his famous last words:

> Crito, we owe a cock to Asclepius. Pay it and do not neglect it. (*Phaedo* 118, tr. H. N. Fowler.)

According to Plato's account, the first and last words spoken by Socrates that day were addressed to Crito.

We cannot be sure what Socrates meant by this cock which the two of them owed to Aesculapius. However, we do know from scenes on vases that a cock — a symbol of male potency — was quite common as a gift in homosexual love relationships. And at the time Crito was certainly a very intimate friend of Socrates. In the opening passage of Plato's dialogue the *Crito* we read for example that he often visited Socrates in prison. The day before the execution he had even been allowed to go in before sunrise (he had bribed the warden). And this same afternoon Socrates had asked Crito — explicitly only Crito — to go with him to the bathroom. Does it not seem obvious to surmise that while the two of them were alone together in the bathroom feelings of lust had arisen and that they had acted on them in a loving and satisfying way? The sacrificial cock to be given to Asclepius might have been a thank offering for the salutary effect of their lovemaking. Whether this was the case or not, Plato ends his account by saying:

> Such was the end of our friend, who was, as we may say, of all those of his time whom we have known, the best and wisest and most righteous man. (*Phaedo* 118, tr. H. N. Fowler.)

Profile of a philosopher

Plato's judgment of Socrates as 'the best and wisest and most righteous man' has become more or less the standard view. As a result, he is exalted almost beyond any criticism. In *Die Grossen Philosophen*, already referred to above, Karl Jaspers even goes as far as to put him on a par with Buddha, Confucius and Jesus. So much veneration will surely go too far for many people; but Jaspers is right when he says that the figure of Socrates has defined the profile of the ideal philosopher.

Originally I agreed with this view — I too was under the spell of his personality as a philosopher and even felt called myself to philosophy. But I could not ignore those short, harrowing passages about Xanthippe and I wondered if, as a woman, I would be able to become a philosopher; perhaps I would be more likely to marry a philosopher and become a Xanthippe myself. Fortunately this was not the way things turned out. How different was my position, two thousand four hundred years later, from Xanthippe's. I could just get on my bicycle, ride to the university and join plenty of other women at the lectures. Nevertheless, I soon discovered that in reality not so much had changed in academic philosophy. Virtually all the lecturers were men. They were in charge and wished to remain so; women did not fit in with the standard profile of the philosopher. The strange thing was that they were completely convinced of the reasonableness and fairness of their judgments, just as Socrates had been. His blind spots had not yet been recognized — and they have still not been recognized today. However, in my opinion the recognition of blind spots in our judgments is a prerequisite for further progress in our search for insight and wisdom.

4
Cicero

Symbol of civilization

Marcus Tullius Cicero, who lived from 106-43 BC, was a famous lawyer and politician who is regarded as the greatest prose writer and philosopher of the Roman republic. His name is widely known; for example, the weekly book supplement of a well-known Dutch newspaper is titled Cicero, so that thousands of Dutch readers see the name every week. The editors had good reasons for choosing this name; Cicero, after all, was the champion of *humanitas* — a term he used to propagate his ideal of humanity and civilization, literary and cultural development, and therefore his name would seem to be an excellent symbol for the supplement of a progressive newspaper which aims to publish articles in these fields.

If we take a closer look we see that things are a little more complicated. Certainly, it cannot be denied that the writings in which Cicero extols his ideal are imposing — in fact so imposing that apparently they sometimes make even academics lose their capacity for critical thought. For example, in his book *Postmoderne moraliteit* (p. 60) Harry Kunneman, professor of humanistics at the Utrecht University, interprets Cicero's humanism as being cosmopolitan in its outlook — a view of humanity extending to the whole human race. While it may be true that the Stoics had this broad perspective, Cicero's view of humanity was definitely not so broad in scope. Moreover, later we will find that even the Stoics' idea of humanity was not really so all encompassing.

To obtain some idea of the difference between Cicero's view of humanity and the concept of humanity on which modern humanism is based we will take a look at his main philosophical work *De Re Publica,* which is clearly a response to Plato's *Politeia*. Both titles can be translated as 'The State' and both authors set out to define the properties of the ideal state. Cicero says that the ideal state can best be realized in the Roman republic, because it is there that his ideal of humanity can best be implemented. In the famous concluding passage the 'Dream of Scipio', which can be regarded as the apotheosis of his work, he writes solemnly and respectfully about three outstanding men who in his opinion had done great service to the Roman republic.

Celebrated heroes

Who were these highly-lauded national heroes? In the first place Scipio Aemilianus. Cicero writes about him in exalted terms, as though presenting a kind of Saviour. He tells us that when this Scipio was a relatively young politician he had had a dream. In this dream he went to heaven (located in the Milky Way) and met several deceased men who had done great service to the Roman state; these men revealed to him the divine mandates which he was to fulfil during his future political career. When he had fulfilled them, he too would be received into that heavenly domain of the elect.

However, if you look at this apotheosis from *De Re Publica* in the light of the historical facts, what you see can hardly be regarded as exemplary models of humanity. For the moment we will ignore the fact that there are no women, slaves, children or 'ordinary men' in Cicero's heaven. But the former governors Scipio Aemilianus meets there, who are so highly extolled by Cicero in this apotheosis — who were they?

They were Scipio Aemilianus' own father, one Aemilius Paullus, and his adoptive grandfather, Scipio Maior. In 168 BC Aemilius Paullus had defeated the Macedonians at Pydna. This took place within the ordinary framework of the imperialistic politics of Rome. However the following year he led a punitive expedition against the population of north-west Greece which even according to the standards of ancient warfare was marked by excessive cruelty. On his orders all the towns and villages were sacked and the population killed or sent into slavery. The deportation of slaves took place on an unparalleled scale: about 150,000 people were enslaved. These achievements certainly testify to excellent management skills, but in our view they are hardly a model of humanity.

The man who guided Scipio Aemilianus around heaven was his adoptive grandfather Scipio Maior, the man who had defeated Carthage in 202 and imposed extremely restrictive peace terms on this trading city in North Africa. But apparently now he regretted being so lenient at the time.

> From a lofty place among the stars, dazzling and brightly lit, he pointed down at Carthage [...]

writes Cicero in prose which sounds so majestic that the revelation of Scipio's future tasks which follows is endowed with a heavenly glow. I will quote just a few phrases from this passage:

> within two years, as a consul, you will utterly lay waste to this city [...] and when you have been elected consul for the second time [...] you will level Numantia [...]. After that, it will be your duty to show your fatherland the light of your character, talent and wisdom [...] All good

citizens, allies and Latins will look to you; you will be the one person on whom the salvation of the country depends (*De Re Publ.* VI. XI and XII).

History teaches us that Scipio Aemilianus got to work very energetically. In 146 he sacked Carthage so drastically that the foundations were only found about a hundred years ago. Any surviving inhabitants were enslaved. In 133 he applied the same methods to the Spanish city of Numantia. In Rome he was known to be a declared opponent of a progressive group led by the brothers Tiberius and Gaius Gracchus. This group had taken pity on Roman citizens who because of the wars and compulsory military service (which lasted from the age of 18 to 46) had been forced to sell their farms to rich landowners and now formed the proletariat of Rome. Tiberius Gracchus submitted an agrarian law which was actually no more than a renewal of an existing law against large-scale land ownership. On account of this attempt to achieve a small measure of social justice for his fellow Roman citizens through legal reform, he was lynched at the assembly of the senate. Scipio Aemilianus was not there personally, but he justified the murder. This was how he showed 'the good citizens' 'the light of his wisdom', for 'the salvation of the country'. In 129 Scipio himself died, probably a victim to his political opponents. It was a bloody period marked by huge social and political differences and civil wars.

This background information shows that in the 'Dream of Scipio' Cicero glorified men who, far from being models of humanity and empathy, according to our standards committed crimes against humanity. Of course we cannot simply apply our own standards to different times and different cultures. Cicero was a writer of stature and put the term 'humanity' on the agenda of our civilization. Nevertheless, we do not need to simply swallow all his fine words and confer merit upon him which he does not deserve.

What he meant by the term 'humanitas' was actually not much more than the distinguished conduct he considered appropriate for the Roman elite; it was certainly not synonymous with our concept of humanity or humanism and there was no question of it applying to all human beings. His words show no empathy and compassion; in fact, they strongly recommend the cruel oppression of any resistance to Roman imperialism and of any struggle for social justice.

Cicero's fellow citizens understood his message well. They were familiar with the names of the heroes celebrated by Cicero and they had a fair idea of the practices associated with them. The large-scale importation of slaves by Aemilius Paullus, the sack of Carthage by Scipio Aemilianus, his opposition of the Gracchi — these were deeds which had had serious economic and social consequences for the Roman population.

For us, more than two thousand years later, the implications of Cicero's words are not immediately obvious. It is only when we have looked these things up in our history books that we realize that when Cicero spoke of 'good citizens' and 'the salvation of the country' he meant something quite different from what we would initially assume. And evidently there are many people who do not realize this — not only teachers and pupils at schools but also academics and journalists. As we have seen, the editors of a newspaper which likes to present itself as progressive chose the name 'Cicero' for its book supplement. It is as though Cicero has been granted a spot in the heaven he himself created, up there in the Milky Way. But the fact that his ideal of *humanitas* does not correspond with our modern views of humanity is often overlooked.

Life and love

In this chapter the relationship between men and women has not yet arisen at all. The primary objective of this book is to discuss several literary highlights from classical antiquity which are still frequently read. The 'Dream of Scipio' is one of these, and no women are mentioned in it. However, it is also interesting to see how our great teachers of ethics lived their own lives and how they thought about and dealt with relationships between men and women; after all, this is an issue which confronts all people of all eras. However, here we have a problem. Although a vast number of written works have survived from antiquity, most of them contain little information about the private lives of the authors: they did not think of this as a suitable topic on which to publish. As a result, in the philosophical texts which are still most frequently read personal aspects play scarcely any role — which is a pity, because ultimately every person's reflection begins with reflection on his or her own life. Starting from their own lives and making comparisons with the lives of others, at other times and in other situations, thinkers can achieve a broader outlook and a higher level of abstraction.

It is also true of Cicero that in most of his works, including the best-known ones, he seldom provided any information about his private life. He was an extremely prolific writer. We have dozens of speeches and dozens of works on oratory and philosophy by Cicero at our disposal. These are the works from which selections for anthologies are usually made — and rightly so, because they contain the literary tours de force. However, fortunately a collection of letters to his friends has also been passed down. (An interesting detail is that the 12-point typographic unit of measure used in the edition of Cicero's letters printed in 1466 is still known as 'cicero'). Some information about

Cicero's private life is to be found in these letters, though more questions remain open than are answered. It was certainly an intriguing life. For the outline below I have made use of the article about Cicero's daughter Tullia written by classicist Wolther Kassies, who took most of his information from Cicero's letters.

Marcus Tullius Cicero was born in 106 BC in Arpinum, a small town in central Italy. He received a good education in Rome, studied there, did military service for a time, which he did not enjoy, began a career as a lawyer and then from 79 to 77 studied in Athens and at Rhodes, university centres of great renown at the time. It must have been shortly after his return to Rome that he married Terentia, who came from a wealthy family, and it was probably about a year later that their daughter Tullia was born. Most marriages at the time were marriages of convenience, so that it is difficult to guess what sort of emotional relationship the spouses might have had. Cicero says nothing about this in his letters to his friends. But it is certain that he loved his daughter Tullia very much.

In 75 BC Cicero began his political career, which meant that he was sometimes away from home for long periods during which he had to leave the management of his financial affairs to Terentia. In 65 their son Marcus was born. In 63 he was appointed consul in Rome. As consul he had several political opponents put to death, with the consent of the senate, but without any form of trial. Of course this was contrary to Roman law and a few years later it gave the opposition an excuse to ban him to Brindisi in southern Italy. It was from this place of exile, in 58, that he wrote the following sentence to Terentia:

> I only wish, my dear, to see you as soon as possible and to die in your arms, since neither gods, whom you have worshipped with such pure devotion, nor men, whom I

have ever served, have made us any return. (*Ep. ad Fam.* 14.4.)

The warmth expressed here — which is remarkable for a classical text — may at the very least serve as an indication that there must have been some good times and a certain depth in his relationship with Terentia. Nevertheless, there is also evidence that at that point the marriage was already waning and that he was not very happy with Terentia's financial management. But there is no doubt that there was a close bond between Cicero and his daughter Tullia. It was she who went to Brindisi to meet him in August 57, when he was given permission to return to Rome from his exile. In the autumn of the same year he wrote to his friend Atticus, discreetly but meaningfully:

> The rest of my concerns are less suited to public knowledge. My brother and my daughter love me. *(Ep. ad Att.* IV.2.7.)

In 54 and 53 he wrote his prestigious work *De Re Publica* (The State), with its famous conclusion the 'Dream of Scipio', which was discussed above; as we saw, no women are mentioned in it. However, in Cicero's personal life during that period there was one woman who was extremely important: his daughter Tullia. She was the greatest and most profound love of his life. In his letters he usually addresses her with various affectionate diminutives ('Tulliola', 'my darling little daughter'), even when she is grown up. At the same time he admires her strength of mind and character and her empathy. For example, he writes to Atticus:

> Her strength of mind is extraordinary. The way she bears the political disaster and domestic vexations [...]

She *is* love, she is the epitome of compassion. (*Ep. ad Att.* x.8.9.)

Probably the words 'domestic vexations' refer to the fact that at that stage Tullia was married to one Dolabella and had just had a seven-month baby, which was not to live for long. This was her third marriage, and it was not a happy one. But they may also be taken in a broader sense: up to that point Tullia's life had certainly not been easy. Her father had arranged her first engagement before she turned twelve. She can scarcely have reached puberty when this first marriage took place. The bridegroom died a few years later. The second marriage Cicero arranged for his daughter was to a man of very distinguished origins, but it soon ended in divorce. Then Tullia and her mother Terentia had organized this third marriage to Dolabella; Cicero had then just taken up a post as proconsul in Cilicia (in present-day Turkey). But Dolabella turned out to be a womanizer and the relationship again failed to bring Tullia happiness.

After his return to Rome Cicero himself had serious marital problems with Terentia. He received a great deal of support from Tullia, with whom he could discuss all his personal affairs. Their bond was stronger than ever. Eventually Cicero divorced Terentia at the end of 47 and shortly after, at the beginning of 46 — when he was 60 years old —, married a teenage girl: his rich ward Publilia. In November of the same year Dolabella divorced Tullia, who was heavily pregnant at the time. She moved in with her father on his property at Tusculum, where her second child, Lentulus, was born in January 45. However, hardly a month later, in February 45, Tullia died from the complications of childbirth. The baby died a few months later.

For Cicero the death of his dearly beloved daughter was a heavy blow. He fell into a severe depression. He sent Publilia away — his second divorce. One source tells us that she had been unable to hide her joy at the death of Tullia, whom she saw as a rival. In his grief he looked for solitude; first in nature — every day he took refuge in a dense and impenetrable forest, returning only in the evening, as he wrote to his friend Atticus in Rome. As much as he could in the face of his grief, he sought comfort in reading books.

But he also made a plan: he wanted to build a little shrine in memory of Tullia. He was completely engrossed in this project — the design, the right location — for quite some time. We do not know if it was ever realized. It is strange that Cicero wanted to erect (and perhaps did erect) a monument in honour of his daughter, whom he loved and admired so much for her empathy when previously, in his 'Dream of Scipio', he had as it were erected a literary monument in honour of heroes who had shown a total lack of this quality.

In the succeeding period Cicero wrote a large number of great philosophical works and made one more appearance in Roman politics. But these were incredibly turbulent times and — like many others — he was put on the notorious 'proscription lists' by his political opponents; in other words, he was outlawed. On 7 December 43 he was killed. His head and hands were nailed to the rostrum at the Roman market where he had had his greatest successes as an orator.

One of the philosophical works Cicero wrote after the death of Tullia was a dialogue titled *Hortensius*; it has now been lost, but we know something about its contents. Apparently this text embodied a striking exhortation to practise philosophy, and thus to renounce all ambitions and physical pleasures. It seems that in this context Cicero expressed a very negative opinion about marriage — an opinion which must have been partly based on his personal experience of marriage relationships, both his own and his daughter's. It was this negative view of marriage which formed the basis of the opinion Cicero expressed in the *Hortensius* — an opinion which became well known — that it is better for a philosopher not to marry. We shall see that after Cicero's death this opinion exercised a strong influence on Augustine — and therefore indirectly on the views still held today in the Catholic church. Could Cicero ever have dreamt that his famous powers of persuasion would have such a long-lasting effect?

5
Seneca

Stoic moralist

Essentially the bloody reality of the civil wars in Cicero's time heralded the end of the Roman republic. The year 27 BC marked the beginning of the Roman Empire. Its beginnings were hopeful; Emperor Augustus managed to restore a reasonable measure of peace, safety and prosperity. But his successors were less competent. The regime of Nero, from 56 to 68, was one of the first low points in the five centuries the empire spanned. It was during this period that a collision took place between the notorious emperor Nero and the famous philosopher Seneca.

Seneca was born in Spain in about 4 BC, but moved to Rome when still a child. In this early period of the Roman Empire he became a successful lawyer, orator, writer and philosopher—a Roman representative of the Stoa, an originally Greek school of philosophy which emphasized compliance with basic moral principles. Seneca was thus a Stoic moralist. Compared with the work of Cicero published about a hundred years earlier, his ethics are a step further along the road to a morality with a wider scope than only the Roman establishment. Seneca's point of view—in a nutshell—is roughly as follows: the whole of humanity shares reason (*ratio*), which is divine in nature. We should therefore all behave in accordance with reason towards everyone, both free men and slaves, and instead of allowing ourselves to be led by emotions strive towards *apatheia*: absence of emotion or absolute self-control.

It was this same Seneca, the great champion of self-control, who became tutor to the cruel, wanton and undisciplined young emperor Nero. Of course this was bound to go wrong — and it did. In 65 Nero, who had first had his own brother poisoned and a few years later also had his mother murdered, sent an order to his teacher Seneca to commit suicide — an order which Seneca could only obey. The Roman historian Tacitus wrote an account of the event as he had heard it from an eye witness. And just as Plato's description of Socrates' forced suicide is still regarded as a highlight of Greek literature, Tacitus' report of Seneca's death is held to be one of the great masterpieces of Latin literature. The passage in question from his *Annals* (xv 60-64) still commands respect and admiration for the man who in this deed provided the ultimate proof of his Stoic attitude to life. Or will it prove possible — in the framework of the unorthodox views on classical texts expressed in this book — to see this story from a slightly different perspective?

End of his life

Let us review the course of events. When Seneca receives the command to commit suicide, he is having dinner with his wife Paulina and a few friends. (The fact that there would also have been many servants present is taken for granted). The house where Seneca and Paulina are staying is already surrounded by soldiers. There is no time for escape or postponement. Alternately chatting amiably and talking seriously, Seneca reprimands his friends for their tears. Then he embraces his wife and tries to give her courage. But she declares that she has decided to die with him. His reaction is:

> I had shown you ways of smoothing life, but you prefer

the glory of death. I will not begrudge you that example. May the fortitude of so courageous an end be equal for us both, but may there be more fame in your decease.

Then the wrists of Seneca and Paulina are cut open with one and the same stroke (*eodem ictu*). They must therefore have been holding their hands and forearms very close together. Because his blood flows so slowly, Seneca also has the arteries of his legs and knees severed. Exhausted by the terrible pain, he advises his wife to go to another room,

> ...afraid that his suffering might break his wife's spirit and that as he looked on her tortures he himself might not be able to persevere.

Then he summons secretaries and dictates long texts, of which Tacitus says in his account that he will not paraphrase them, because they have already been published.

Because the process of death is taking so long, Seneca sends a friend to fetch some poison he had procured a long time before — the same drug which was used to poison Socrates. But it turns out that it does not work, because it can no longer be taken into his blood. Finally he gets into a pool of heated water and sprinkles the nearest of his slaves, adding the exclamation: 'I offer this water as a libation to Jupiter the Deliverer'. He is then carried to a steam bath and after he has been suffocated by the steam he is cremated without any funeral rites, as he had requested in a codicil.

Proof of apatheia

It is immediately clear that while there are similarities between the accounts of Socrates' and Seneca's deaths, there are also striking differences. Both were forced to end their lives. Socrates swallowed the poison himself, so that his death really was forced suicide. Seneca did not cut his own veins; sometimes this is claimed, but the Latin text does not allow such an interpretation: Seneca could hardly have cut his own wrists and Paulina's with one and the same stroke. Apparently he burdened someone else (probably a slave) with this task. It was therefore not suicide in the strict sense; you might say that to a large extent he directed the implementation of his own death sentence — his own murder.

Both sent their wives away. But what a difference! In a previous chapter we saw how detached Socrates was when he sent Xanthippe away. Seneca's warm embrace may compensate for his somewhat condescending tone ('I had shown you...'). However, it is curious that he interprets Paulina's decision to join him in death as a means of achieving glory. You would think that her prime motivation would have been to express her love for him and solidarity with his fate. It is not impossible that the thought of glory played a role for her, but we do not know if this was the case. Seneca's assumption that it was says more about his own goal than his wife's.

And then: his solemn promise that he will not begrudge her the example of a glorious death, followed by his solemnly pronounced wish that her death may win more fame. Did he keep this promise, and how sincere was his wish? Of course it is completely understandable that he loses his *apatheia* when the pain becomes too severe and that he is afraid his resolve will weaken. But to project his own fear onto Paulina and to assume that she too will lose her fortitude is hardly fair. The fact that he advised her to go to another room — which was apparently regarded as a command and obeyed — does not show much loyalty; in fact, in doing so he puts an end to their shared journey towards death. She has to leave the stage and is excluded; he assumes the leading role in the show. Ultimately he did begrudge her the glory of 'that example of fortitude of so courageous an end', to use some of his own terms.

After her departure he suddenly regains enough energy to dictate long texts to his secretaries, just as Socrates had lengthy conversations with his friends in the hours preceding his death. There is a bath in this story too, and at the last minute, a sacrifice to a god with an element of humour — just before an abrupt end. This all suggests a deliberate imitation of Socrates.

The death of Seneca has always been regarded as the glorious and overwhelming proof of his *apatheia*. But his words to Paulina betray his real ambition: it was glory he was after, at least as much glory as Socrates had achieved. He must have been cherishing this plan to match Socrates for quite some time — he had procured the poison long before he needed it. Perhaps he even wanted to score points off Socrates with his warm embrace of Paulina, but her unexpected desire to share his death thwarted his plan. At first he reacts chivalrously, but her decision does not really fit in with his hidden agenda: he wants to work on one last publication and does not want her presence and the sight of her in the throes of death upsetting this work. Like Socrates, Seneca sends his wife away.

In my view Seneca's death was not the ultimate proof of his *apatheia* and indifference to death, but of his ambition and desire for glory. He also revealed himself as an egocentric and short-sighted husband — because by sending his wife away he deprived both of them of the authentic experience which love and a shared lot can provide in an extreme situation. Together they could have given a unique example to humanity and gained well-deserved glory into the bargain. A lost opportunity.

Paulina

Who was Paulina and what happened to her? Once again: we know very little about the wives of most of the famous men of antiquity. She was the second — much younger — wife of Seneca and she does not appear to have had any children.

Tacitus tells us that when Nero heard about Paulina's attempt to choose her own death, he ordered her veins to be bandaged so as to prevent her from dying. This was successful. She lived a few more years, in praiseworthy remembrance of her husband. But what she herself thought, we will never know.

Stoic ideal

Let us take another look at Seneca's ideal: *apatheia*. It is from this Greek word that our word 'apathy' is derived, but it has a somewhat different meaning. Apathy suggests both listlessness and idleness. Seneca's *apatheia* literally means lack of emotion; it aims for total self-control, which may, however, go hand in hand with an intellectually active approach to life. Seneca himself wrote many works. He bases his idea of *apatheia* on divine reason, *ratio*, which is shared by all human beings and according to which all human beings should live. He condemns all forms of unreasonable behaviour: war, gladiator games, cruelty — including cruelty to slaves. However, he does not condemn slavery itself, because the situation in which you find yourself is irrelevant; it is something outside yourself, to which you should be indifferent. *Ratio* and *apatheia* make you free and independent; they enable you to close yourself off from everything outside you, whether you are a master or a slave. And if your concrete situation becomes unbearable, you can always put an end to it by committing suicide.

In his *Letters to Lucilius* Seneca gives various examples of self-elected death, for instance in his letter about a Spartan boy called Marcellinus. This boy had been taken captive but was not willing to live as a slave; so the very first time he was ordered to perform a menial task — he had to fetch a chamber-pot — he dashed out his brains against the wall.

> So near at hand is freedom, and is anyone still a slave? (*Ep. ad Luc.* 77.15.)

was Seneca's rhetorical question. But is this extreme position really so rational? It certainly does not show much sense of reality. To reach such a degree of freedom and independence through *apatheia* is rather a lot to ask from so many thousands of slaves — both male and female — and all the other poor wretches who constantly lived in extremely difficult circumstances.

At the beginning of this same letter Seneca, himself enormously wealthy, shows that he was quite impressed with his own feats of *apatheia*. When he was standing on the jetty at an Italian harbour and saw mailboats arriving from Egypt, which would be bringing him news about his overseas estates, he had not been curious at all about the revenue they had generated! For him, the cultivation of *apatheia* generally meant no more than an exercise in the art of living, free of obligations; it was only incidentally that it gained an existential dimension. But for the slaves who had to work beneath the burning Egyptian sun on his estates, or who sat rowing on the tiny oarsmen's benches in the mailboats, it was an existential necessity to bear their lot with *apatheia* every day of their lives. It is doubtful whether this made them feel very free and independent.

Empathy

As we have seen, according to Seneca we must all behave towards all others in accordance with divine *ratio*. This suggests an ideal of a universal community of reason and justice. While he does condemn various forms of cruelty, his interpretation of rationality is actually limited to the ideal of *apatheia*. In his view you should shut off your feelings from everything outside yourself and aspire to independence from all external factors. In other words, he does not advocate active participation in or attempts to combat wrongdoing, but passive acceptance of it. He suggests that by using *apatheia* as protective armour and as a panacea, everyone, in all circumstances, will be adequately armed against all evil and injustice.

Seneca seems to overlook the fact that human beings —all human beings—are dependent on care, at some stages of life—for example as infants or in illness—more than at others. During a dependent phase *apatheia* is not always to be recommended. And Seneca himself, who liked to present himself as being independent, simply took it for granted that there were people around to serve him and take care of him. As a rule, in his circles these people were women and slaves—both male and female. Obviously they could not close themselves off in complete *apatheia* from the wishes and feelings of their masters. There is no doubt that they had to be aware of their own feelings in order to empathize with the needs of others and satisfy them. Following this line of reasoning, you might expect empathy to be an indispensable component of the divine rationality which was supposed to guide the behaviour of all people towards all others. However, Seneca's *apatheia* strives toward complete control or even elimination of feelings and leaves very little room for empathy. In my opinion it is precisely empathy which might have added a dimension of human commitment to his ideal of rationality, transforming it into the pursuit of a justice which would truly have applied to all human beings with respect to all other human beings, including women and slaves.

Admittedly, Seneca's ideal of *apatheia* does have a positive side. In emergencies it is helpful to be able to control yourself, to eliminate your feelings temporarily and to act according to your reason. But Seneca's ideal was the permanent repression of all emotions which might disturb one's equilibrium. This implies not only cutting yourself off from the depth of your own feelings, but also from the feelings of others. What it boils down to is enclosing yourself in egocentricity.

Obviously this attitude would make an impact on a marriage, among other areas of life. According to Seneca, a wise man should by no means love his wife passionately. Passion itself is an excess, but by excessively loving someone outside yourself your soul might lose control of itself. And in his tragedy *Medea*, for example, he exuberantly depicted the terrible excesses that could lead to.

This tragedy by Seneca is based on the same story as the much more widely known tragedy of the same name written nearly five hundred years earlier by the Greek playwright Euripides. The story is about Medea, who runs away with her beloved Jason and gives up everything for him, but is ultimately betrayed by him and takes revenge in a horrific way. The American classicist and philosopher Martha Nussbaum presents an outstanding analysis of Seneca's version in her essay 'Serpents in the Soul: A Reading of Seneca's *Medea*'. Nussbaum makes the crucial difference between Seneca and Euripides very clear: whereas Euripides has a positive attitude to love and calls it the most delightful thing there is so long as it does not get out of hand, Seneca asserts that excess is inherent in love, because in love you make yourself dependent on erotic passion. In his view a person should steer clear of it and maintain Stoic independence by means of *apatheia*.

It seems an obvious conclusion that Seneca's ideal of *apatheia* was actually nurtured by an intense fear of his own feelings. Out of fear that he would not be able to control his feelings in all circumstances, he thought he should control them constantly or eliminate them. How completely different this is from the view commonly accepted today that life itself undeniably also depends on emotional competence. In human existence you start with emotions. It is only from that starting point that the process of guidance by means of reason can begin.

While most people will not see the application of Seneca's *apatheia* as a realistic option for shaping their marriages, it is of no use at all to people who take it upon themselves to care for other people who are dependent on help. This kind of care is impossible without emotional involvement and empathy. In short, for most people even if Seneca's ideal of *apatheia* were attainable in practice, it would not be a very appealing or helpful attitude to life.

In the course of the centuries there has been some criticism of Seneca's life and doctrine, but admiration has predominated, and his death is still regarded as the ultimate proof of his *apatheia* and as a triumph of reason over the emotions. But read in a different light, the same text about the end of his life seems to suggest that ambition and fear were the factors which caused him to violate his solemn declaration to Paulina and their agreement to end their lives together. From this perspective a more apt interpretation of the way Seneca's life ended is that it was a proof that emotions are driving forces which cannot be repressed. And many will be more inclined to conclude that it is much wiser to discern and acknowledge emotions, and to bring them into balance with the help of reason.

I would not go as far as the classicist Piet Schrijvers, who wrote in an exam preparation textbook that a bust of Seneca would be an appropriate adornment in an American psychotherapy clinic because he might be regarded as one of the inspirers of Rational Emotive Behaviour Therapy, which tries to combat negative emotions by means of rational argumentation. I think it might be somewhat misleading in this context to honour a man who inspired so many people throughout so many centuries to cherish the one-sided and unhealthy ideal of repressing emotions. For this is certainly the case: the Stoic ideal of repression of the emotions by means of rationality has fascinated and inspired many throughout the centuries, particularly men. However the ideal is manifested — from the 'stiff upper lip' to the cowboy maxim that 'a man has to do what a man has to do' (usually followed by a shot) — men like to excel in it. And in some circles this attitude still meets with approval or is regarded as 'cool', although many people now have different views.

6
Augustine

Youth

In the late Roman Empire Christianity — amidst various other religious streams — was rapidly growing in popularity. In 354 AD one Augustine was born into this mixture of beliefs and ideologies. His place of birth was Thagaste, a minor provincial town in the north African mountain area of Numidia, which was part of the Roman Empire. He was the son of Patricius, a tax collector who adhered to the traditional Roman polytheistic religion, and Monica, a devout Christian. This Augustine came to be perhaps the most influential of all the Church fathers. Even today his views still exert an influence in what ex-priest James Carroll calls the 'sexual totalitarianism' of the Catholic church. We have every reason to extract a few personal details from Augustine's enormous oeuvre which may have been relevant to the formation of his views on this subject. For this purpose I have made use of the biography of Augustine by the American historian Garry Wills which was published in 1999.

Destined by his father for an administrative position, Augustine was given a good education, first in Thagaste, later in a town a little further away. When he was about sixteen he entered into a relationship with a Christian girl; we do not know her name. At about seventeen he went to study in Carthage. (As we saw in a previous chapter, Carthage had been completely destroyed in 146 BC, but in the meantime a new town of the same name had sprung up in the same area and was prospering.) The young couple lived there together. They were not officially married; this situation was not unusual at the time, and in fact a liaison of this kind even had legal status. They had a son called Adeodatus, which literally means 'given by God'; in his biography *Saint Augustine* Garry Wills refers to the boy as 'Godsend'. Augustine's father Patricius died and shortly afterwards his mother Monica came to live with the young family in Carthage.

Even in his student days Augustine was fascinated by authors such as Plato, Cicero and Virgil. These authors were to have a permanent influence on his later work. To the disappointment of his mother he became a Manichaean. The followers of Manichaeism revered a man called Mani, whom they regarded as the son of God, sent by God to the world, whereas to Christ they attributed the more abstract role of the light sent by God to mankind. In the Catholic church, which was already quite highly organized and to which Monica belonged, this movement was regarded as heretical and sectarian.

Social success

After completing his studies Augustine became a teacher, first in Thagaste, the town of his birth, and then in Carthage. However, he was completely incapable of keeping order. When he heard that pupils in Rome were more docile he decided in 383 AD, when he was 29 years old, to move to Italy with his mistress and child—without informing Monica.

In Rome he had no success as a teacher either. However, in 384 he was offered an excellent job which seemed to match his training and capacities better: he became court orator at Milan. In this position he did very well, and soon he was leading a sizeable household, which by then his mother Monica had also joined. Because Augustine had now climbed so much higher on the social ladder, she then arranged an engagement for him to a girl from a good background. The girl was only ten years old. Since the reign of Emperor Augustus, the minimum age at which girls could marry had been raised to twelve, so that the marriage could not take place at once. However, the engagement was not solely the result of social considerations; a fundamental rejection of sexuality must also have been a factor, because Monica and Augustine shared the hope that with such a young girl as his wife he would be able to abstain from sex.

Repudiation of his mistress

Partly under the influence of the views expressed by Cicero in his *Hortensius* — which has been lost — Augustine had come to believe that a philosopher should lead a chaste life and abstain from sex. And because he thought he would be unable to do this within his relationship with the woman he had loved for nearly fifteen years, he sent her back to Africa. He kept Adeodatus, his 'gift from God', with him, because at that time a child was regarded as the property of its father. Nevertheless it seems rather contradictory that he kept his gift from God while sending away the person through whom he had received this gift. Augustine, who had such a strong bond with his own mother Monica, took his son's mother away from him and deprived the mother of her son. Evidently he had not yet grasped the Christian message:

> And as you wish that men would do to you, do so to them. (Luke 6.31.)

He found separation from his mistress difficult. In his *Confessions* he wrote:

> When the woman I had been used to sleeping with was torn from my side [...], my heart [...] was lacerated and wounded and kept bleeding. (*Conf.* 6.25.)

The passive phrase 'was torn from my side' seems to reveal that he himself had not been the main driving force behind the dismissal of his mistress. And in fact it had been Monica's idea; but of course Augustine himself was entirely responsible for the decision.

It is impossible to justify this dismissal. Augustine's biographer Wills does not explicitly try to justify it either, but he does soften its impact by asking:

> But can we say that he 'dismissed her'? She presumably had some say in the matter, and looked to her son's prospects as well as her own peace of soul. (*Saint Augustine*, p. 41.)

Then Wills goes into all sorts of speculations about possible motives she may have had for the separation and about places where she may later have lived with her family in Africa. His conclusion sounds more certain:

> At any rate, she would have remained in correspondence with Godsend. (*Saint Augustine*, p. 42.)

These are all touching and speculative utterances about the thoughts and fate of a woman about whom we know nothing at all — not even her name. It is therefore better to limit ourselves to the sober conclusion that at that time the social position of a woman who had been cast out was extremely weak. As a rule such a woman would not have been welcomed with open arms by her relatives. We do not know if she was able to stay in touch with her son, but it is not very likely.

Conversion and celibacy

To Monica's joy, in 386 Augustine converted to Christianity, which since 380 had been the state religion in the whole Roman Empire. For practical reasons his baptism did not take place immediately. He probably broke off his relationships with the young girl and with another woman — an interim girlfriend — at that point, and it was around the same time that he made the final decision to live a completely celibate life:

> I have resolved that there is nothing I should shun so much as sexual intercourse; I think that nothing casts down the mind of man from its citadel more than the seductions of a woman and the physical intimacy without which a wife cannot be possessed. (*Soliloquia* 1.x.17.)

This statement is from his *Soliloquia*, a singular work in which Augustine examines himself in a dialogue with his own reason (*ratio*). In the passage quoted above Augustine attributes sexual seduction one-sidedly to women. He also talks about 'possessing' a wife. Anyone who 'possesses' someone also has power over that person and is thus able to compel that person to have a relationship, with or without a sexual component. The wife can attempt to seduce her husband, whereas the husband can force his wife one way or the other.

It would therefore be more realistic to ascribe the compulsion of sexual seduction at least partly to Augustine's own feelings of lust. After all, the fact that he had sent his own mistress away had apparently not delivered him from his own libido. But now he wants to elevate that libido to a higher and more spiritual level, as we read a little further in the text, when in conjunction with his reason he tries to analyse his love of wisdom. His reason says:

> Now we will inquire what kind of a lover you are of that Wisdom, whom you desire to behold and grasp with completely chaste regard and embrace, without any veil, as though she were naked, in a way she does not permit except to very few of her choicest lovers. (*Soliloquia* 1. XIII.22.)

The next passage is about Augustine's method of attaining his goal of 'beholding Wisdom'. This method was partly inspired by Plato's well-known cave simile: climbing up further and further from the obscure and earthly until one can see the brightest heavenly light, the sun itself. But his *ratio* makes things difficult for him, sometimes even reducing him to tears:

> How low, how execrable, how cursed, how horrible a woman's embrace seemed to you, when we were discussing between ourselves concerning the desire for a wife! And yet this very night, when we were awake and again reflecting on these things, you noticed how those imaginary seductions and bitter sweetness aroused you — otherwise than you had assumed; far, far less than in reality, but yet quite differently than you had thought. (*Soliloquia* 1.XIV.25.)

It will be obvious to the modern reader that there was nothing wrong with Augustine's libido in itself, but that the renunciation of these physical pleasures and his attempt to elevate them to a higher spiritual level meant a great struggle for him — a struggle which in our times would probably be seen as an obstruction to harmonious personal development.

The fact that the repression of his feelings of sexual lust was very difficult for him is also shown by a passage in his *Confessions*, which were written later. A quotation from Wills's biography (*Saint Augustine* p. 46):

In his agony, Augustine imagines a personified Self-Control (*Continentia*) islanded off from him in a place he fears to enter. She 'reaches out hands of affection toward me, to receive and embrace me' — Virgil's image is vaguely present, of souls that yearn for a far shore, 'stretching hands toward it'. (*Aeneid* 6.314.) The appearance of Self-Control is something that occurs 'in my own heart, pitting myself against myself'. (*Confessions* 8.27.)

However, no matter how difficult Augustine's struggle may have been, he is firmly resolved that he wants nothing more to do with the 'seductive Eve' type of woman.

Vision shared with his mother

On the other hand the bond between Augustine and his mother Monica was growing stronger and stronger. Monica took part in the philosophical discussions Augustine had with a few friends and his son, and his admiration for her grew steadily. In 387 Monica's long-cherished wish was fulfilled: Augustine was baptized. Shortly afterwards he resigned from his distinguished job in Milan and set out to return to Africa. His son Adeodatus and Monica were included in the small group accompanying him. When they reached the port of Ostia, the intimate relationship between mother and son reached its climax in a shared vision.

The description of this vision is a well-known highlight of Augustine's work. It is famous not only for its exceptional content — a spiritual experience shared by two people in which they are elevated above and beyond themselves and for one short moment see wisdom itself — but also for its exceptional literary form, culminating in one sentence which lasts a whole page. Here is just a fragmented passage:

> Imagine that the tumult of the flesh were silenced for some man; [...] that every transient thing were silenced for him [...] if then He alone spoke, [...] not in fleshly tongue [...] but that we might hear Him whom we love in created things without those created things, as we strained ourselves and in one rapid flash of thought touched on the eternal wisdom which endures beyond all — imagine that this could be sustained [...] so that there would be an eternally lasting life of the same nature as that one moment of insight which we yearned for — would this not be the reality of the saying: 'Enter into the joy of your Lord?' (*Conf.* IX, 25.)

In the eyes of many believers this vision which Augustine shared with Monica still commands awe, as though it were a sublimated union of the son Augustine, the mother Monica and God the Father. Others are inclined to take a different point of view and to see it as a regrettable culmination of a symbiotic relationship between mother and son, in which the experience of sexual pleasure is classified as sin and which has destroyed any possibility of a normal healthy sexual life for the son as well as the love relationship he had with his de facto wife. In the history of the Catholic church this negative view of sexuality played a major role in the development of a sexual morality which is still influential today.

Bishop

Soon after their shared vision Monica died. In 388 Augustine and his son settled in Africa for good; however, Adeodatus died shortly after. Augustine, although he had only been baptized two years earlier, was soon ordained a priest and a few years later became a bishop. His piety and his commitment as a pastor commanded great respect. It is interesting to see that in his exhortations to future priests he always emphasized the importance of sympathy (*Saint Augustine* p. 73):

> For if you minister to the sick, you become sick yourself, not by pretending to have the same fever, but because you consider, with the mind of one truly sympathizing, how you would wish to be treated if you were sick yourself. (*Epistulae* 40.4.)

However, not only had Augustine himself failed to show empathy towards his own de facto wife in the past, but considering that the ideal of marriage which he held up to his congregation was 'affection without sex' he also failed to incorporate empathy into his views on married life and sexuality.

From that point onwards Augustine grew to be one of the most prolific writers of all times. When he died in 430 at the age of 76, his oeuvre was many times larger than that of Cicero. Cicero wrote dozens of minor and major works, but Augustine wrote hundreds. Like many authors in antiquity, he did not actually write his texts himself but dictated them to stenographers. It is fairly easy to work out that because he 'wrote' such an incredible amount and must also have slept sometimes, he cannot have been alone very often and must have been talking almost all the time. Many think that his immense oeuvre still makes compelling reading — but in my opinion it also contains a curious imbalance.

Autobiography

Augustine's two best-known works are his *Confessions,* on which he worked approximately from the age of 43 to 46 and *De Civitate Dei* (The City of God), written at a more advanced age. This is actually his most important work; it will be mentioned again in the last chapter of this book. Here I will limit myself to a short discussion of the *Confessions*, an autobiography in the form of a long prayer consisting of thirteen books. In this work Augustine renders an account of the life he has led thus far, his views on his spiritual life and the story of creation. Most of the biographic details given above are taken from this work.

It is striking that in the *Confessions* Augustine devotes a great deal of space to his mother Monica — her youth, her marriage, her death — but is extremely brief when it comes to the woman he had lived with for nearly fifteen years as a young man. He does not mention her name. While he says he was faithful to her all those years: 'unam habebam' (I had only one woman), he goes on to state frankly that after he had sent her away he had had another mistress for some time. The two words 'unam habebam' inspired Garry Wills to name Augustine's de facto wife 'Una' so as to 'avoid clumsy titles' (*Saint Augustine* p. 16). I prefer to regard this omission of her name as significant and to respect it.

Suppression of the names of wives and mistresses is not uncommon, particularly in biblical contexts, but Augustine's deeper motivation was probably the fact that he had sent his mistress away and wanted to forget her. And his readers are also supposed to forget her. But who can forget this woman, who in the security of their shared love and the child they had had together travelled across the seas with her partner to a distant land and a better future — surely every woman who has committed herself to a man will identify with her? And when Augustine complains that his heart was torn apart by their separation, how can you fail to wonder what happened to her heart? For she was not only cast aside by her partner, but also deprived of her son and of the social protection she enjoyed as Augustine's de facto wife.

Influence on the church

Both Monica and Augustine were canonized. Augustine is regarded as one of the most influential Church Fathers of Western Christianity. While he was certainly not the only man to renounce sexuality and regard a celibate life as the most appropriate for priests, because he had so much authority he made a major contribution to the sexual morality of the Catholic church, according to which women are inferior and sexual pleasure sinful, and only male priests leading celibate lives may represent God on earth. This is an attitude which still prevails in the church today.

In his article 'From celibacy to godliness' in the *Boston Globe* (04.09.2004) James Carroll refers to this view as 'sexual totalitarianism'. In this article the ex-priest focuses primarily on compulsory celibacy for priests, but also discusses the views of the Catholic church on sexuality in a more general sense:

> ...what I have come to understand, over the last 25 years as a husband and father, is that sexual engagement, the reciprocity of marriage, and the creativity of parenthood are fundamental sources of engagement with God. [...] The Vatican's dishonesty on all matters concerned with sex — no birth control, no condoms for AIDS prevention, etc. — is now fully perceived by the Catholic people. Sexual totalitarianism will no longer succeed as an organizing principle of this institution.

Time will show whether this optimistic conclusion is justified.

7
Fame or blame: a recapitulation

It is not only reading and writing that are selective processes: judgments are evidently also a matter of selection. Whether we base our judgments on our own subjective selection of the data found in the text or follow the selection and judgments of some external authority, judgments are always characterized by subjectivity.

In my view Homer's character Calypso should have become famous for her criticism of the double standard and for her moral principle in which empathy and rationality are the main ingredients, while she herself also gave a striking demonstration of the magnanimity this principle sometimes demands in practice. But instead she was blamed for sharing her bed with Odysseus. In the history of ethics Calypso's message is never mentioned. In the next chapter, in a section about the exclusion of a whole series of women philosophers from the history of philosophy, I will explain why Calypso might be called a 'literary prototype' of women philosophers.

Socrates is usually regarded as the founder of ethics. With his intellectualistic approach to virtue he put full emphasis on reason; his view — one usually referred to as 'Socratic determinism' — was that anyone who knows what is right will behave in accordance with that knowledge. Socrates himself is seen as an exemplary philosopher in whom thought and action, theory and practice were in complete harmony: a model of rationality and justice. This image of Socrates has defined the profile of the ideal philosopher.

FAME OR BLAME: A RECAPITULATION

Socrates' wife Xanthippe was accused of being unreasonably ill-tempered and reputed to be an impossible woman. As we have seen, there were some flaws in Socrates' rationality and justice, and Xanthippe's indignation had rational grounds. It was not so much that she was an impossible woman, but that she was burdened with an impossible task, which she nevertheless performed with commitment and empathy. Apparently Socrates did not realize that she had rational grounds for her anger. He remained convinced that he had never wronged anyone or failed in his duty, whereas in reality he did fail in his duty; not only did he fail to have empathy with Xanthippe, but he also failed in his concrete obligations to her and their children, obligations which he had consciously assumed in spite of his calling.

Many people believe that the famous Roman orator and philosopher Cicero, with his ideal of humanity, embodies an ideal of civilization and solidarity. But as we saw, his fine words are deceptive. Cicero was convinced that his ideal of humanity could best be implemented in his own Roman republic; but in reality this was a republic which pursued iron-fisted conservative and imperialistic policies. An investigation of the heroes glorified by Cicero in his 'Dream of Scipio' in the light of the historical facts reveals a shocking picture of Cicero himself, who, in his fervent patriotism, venerated heroes who showed no empathy or compassion whatsoever with the victims of those policies, whether they were adversaries or citizens of the Roman state itself. These heroes celebrated by Cicero contrasted starkly with his daughter Tullia whom he loved and adored so much and for whom he wanted to erect a shrine — in memory of her loving character and her empathy. The strange thing is that the 'Dream of Scipio' is still read today, but that editions of the text rarely make any mention of its moral implications. Reading Cicero's texts from a different angle reveals the suffering of thousands of people which is not mentioned by Cicero but is implicit in the texts; it may therefore also lead us to revise our judgments.

Although at least Seneca's ideal went beyond an oppressive nationalism and his ethics did in fact have a cosmopolitan dimension, the concept of empathy was not on his list of desirable qualities. In his opinion every human being should be able to cope with every situation with the help of his rationalistic ideal of *apatheia*, complete control of the emotions. Many still see the much-read and much-praised account of his own forced suicide as a triumph of reason over emotions — the ultimate proof that Seneca himself was a master of self-control. But to me the text conveys that his overwhelming motivation was a desire for glory — a glory in which there was no room for his wife. Like Xanthippe, Paulina had to disappear from the scene.

In Augustine's thinking, the crucial role played by rationality in the ethics of philosophers such as Socrates, Cicero and Seneca is only partly taken over by religion. He compares favourably with these older philosophers in that he regards empathy as an essential ingredient in the work of a shepherd of souls. But his repudiation of his own de facto wife and his views on sexuality show not so much philosophical insight as a lack of self-insight and a lack of empathy towards his fellow human beings.

Socrates, Cicero, Seneca and Augustine became renowned for their achievements in the field of ethics and have been praised for their rationality. However, in many respects their personal lives and theories reflect egocentricity and lack of empathy. They all had double standards. In the texts we have examined, details about their relationships with women reveal an incapacity in all of them to develop balanced views, not only with respect to their own wives and their own marriages, but also with respect to women in general and women's position in society. You might say that these leading authorities on moral philosophy had a blind spot in their perception of humanity where women were concerned. Blind spots are not necessarily alarming — every era has its own blind spots. But it is important to identify and discuss them; otherwise we run the risk of hearing only the positive elements in the ideas of these teachers of ethics, while the negative characteristics also continue to have normative effects.

8
Women and the history of philosophy

Philosophy — a male monopoly

In the previous chapters I have discussed several texts from Greek and Latin literature and philosophy. These are texts which are still often read, and also taught at schools — as they should be, since they are literary highlights. But these texts also have significant moral and philosophical implications. The strange thing is that both at schools and in classics departments at universities these philosophical implications are often overlooked. The traditional commentaries usually focus on linguistic details or the stylistic properties of the texts.

To give an example I will go back to the passage from Cicero's 'Dream of Scipio' in which the young Scipio is shown the city of Carthage from the star-lit sky. In my textbook on the history of Latin literature, written by the Dutch scholar P. J. Enk, the author referred to it as 'this exceptionally beautiful passage [...] as though it were organ music'. A few lines further in the text we read: 'within two years, as a consul, you will utterly lay waste to this city'. And this is exactly what happened: in 146 BC the hero glorified by Cicero razed the prosperous trading city of Carthage to the ground. At the time it must have been a horrifying event — perhaps comparable with the atomic bomb dropped on Hiroshima. However, not only did Cicero himself fail to devote a single word of his text to the moral implications of this historical event; the commentaries of school and university textbooks usually also ignore them. They present Cicero as a great writer and an important philosopher, and his contribution to civilization is stressed over and over again; but any discussion of the moral implications of his political philosophy seems to be almost taboo.

Not only the philosophers' main political standpoints but also their personal lives could do with a little more critical attention, especially at schools, where we deal with young people who are just beginning to consciously shape their own lives. But in university textbooks the personal lives of philosophers are usually regarded as insignificant and irrelevant to the study of these important and authoritative authors. And naturally this view is passed on at secondary schools.

Wilhelm Windelband's *The History of Philosophy*, one of the most famous textbooks on the subject which was the standard work at many universities — also in their classical philosophy departments — throughout the twentieth century, touches on the personal lives of philosophers as briefly as possible and only in small case. It contains just one reference to the relationship between Socrates and Xanthippe:

> He regarded it as his duty and his divine calling, even neglecting the care of his family (Xanthippe), to provide himself and his fellow citizens with insight into the worthlessness of false knowledge and to conduct serious research into the truth (1, 2, 6).

The fact that Socrates' 'divine calling' must have preceded his deliberate choice to start a family has been overlooked and therefore not mentioned. The reference to Xanthippe here is practically the only time a woman's name is mentioned in the whole thick book — and it is in brackets and in small case. Women philosophers are not mentioned at all.

In his famous book *Die grossen Philosophen* (The Great Philosophers, 1956), Karl Jaspers postulates a fundamentally different view of the relationship between theory and personal life; he discusses the topic of 'work and personality' at length, claiming that there is always interaction between an individual's work and private life. In his opinion truly great philosophers are characterized by the consistency between their work and their private lives. He considers Socrates to be one of the four greatest and most influential philosophers of humanity — along with Buddha, Confucius and Jesus. In Jaspers there is not a word to be found about any possible friction between theory and practice in Socrates' life. On the contrary: his behaviour is idealized. It was already mentioned above that Jaspers saw the last encounter between Socrates and Xanthippe as 'a friendly farewell'.

Of course these textbooks by Windelband and Jaspers are now out of date and one might assume that by now the changed views on women and the views of women themselves have been integrated into the disciplines of the classics and philosophy. But this is simply not the case. For example, a textbook by Hans Joachim Störig which is today accessible to a wide public and is often used at universities in several countries deals with the relationship between Socrates and Xanthippe in just one sentence, which is completely in line with Windelband and Jaspers:

> But he soon began to neglect the trade he had learnt from his father and also his family — the reproaches of his wife Xanthippe are proverbial — in order to devote himself entirely to teaching; he felt he was called to do so and no-one before him had ever done it as he did.

The authors of these standard works constantly follow in each other's footsteps and even at the beginning of the twenty-first century they do not stop for a moment to consider whether Xanthippe may have had rational grounds for her anger. Later in this chapter we will see that Störig's book almost completely ignores women in other contexts as well — both as philosophical thinkers and as objects of philosophical thought.

Until recently academic philosophy was almost completely in the hands of men. It is therefore men's interpretations which are presented to us and men have in fact had the monopoly in the formation of value judgments concerning the surviving texts. It seems very likely that it was precisely because they could identify with their great models from history that it was so easy for them to overlook their blind spots. It has not been uncommon for philosophers, in their attempts to imitate their illustrious predecessors, to copy the less laudable aspects of their conduct as well. The exclusion of women from philosophy in classical antiquity had consequences for centuries; its impact can still be seen today in the numerical representation of women and men in academic philosophy.

However, fortunately there are now many male philosophers who are not happy with the situation as it is. For example, in his beautiful book *Sophie's World* Jostein Gaarder discusses the history of philosophy in a very original way, setting out to stimulate young women in particular to engage in philosophy. But even he falls victim to the selection process in current philosophy textbooks: his huge admiration for Socrates is not tempered by any criticism, he mentions only one woman from the whole of classical antiquity (Diotima), and while in comparison to Windelband, Jaspers and Störig he pays quite a lot of attention to views on women and to women philosophers, if the facts relating to these topics had been more readily available he would indubitably have offered more information about them. My discussion of Calypso (see later in this chapter) as a 'literary prototype' of a series of women philosophers throughout history will provide some supplementary information.

Gaarder also fails to explain satisfactorily how the exclusion of women from philosophy was effected. One of the aims of this study is to shed more light on the process as it took place in classical antiquity. To illustrate this I will go back to the quotation from Socrates cited earlier in this book, in which he claims that

> to talk every day about virtue and the other things about which you hear me talking and examining myself and others is the greatest good to man, and that the unexamined life is not worth living. (*Apol.* 38a, tr. H.N. Fowler.)

On the face of it, this phrase looks like a splendid justification for a life spent as a fulltime philosopher. But readers tend to overlook the fact that this striking generic statement did not really refer to 'man' in the sense of 'all mankind' and that as a rule large groups of people, including all women, were excluded from such a life as a matter of course. In my textbooks I never came across this criticism. Presumably I was not the only one to doubt, after reading a passage like this as a schoolgirl, if a life like this would ever be possible for a woman. Recognition of the blind spot in these words of Socrates should be a good reason for all philosophers to keep an eye on generic usage of the term 'man' and to ask themselves to whom it really refers and who might be excluded.

Women philosophers

If you take a look at the indexes of textbooks on the history of philosophy, in most cases you will find that practically no women are mentioned. Recent academic research has, however, shown that in the course of history there have been a large number of women philosophers. To give some examples of where information about these philosophers can be found: in the last decade of the past century, the American philosopher Mary Ellen Waithe, in a four volume work titled *A History of Women Philosophers*, presented dozens of women philosophers from all eras of history. Before that, in 1980, Mary Warren published the excellent *The Nature of Woman. An Encyclopedia and Guide to the Literature*. It is shameful to realize that the history of philosophy, a discipline which sets out to find universally valid insights, has been a history of apartheid. But partly thanks to the books of Waithe and Warren, now at least I can fulfil my promise and explain my characterization of Calypso as the 'literary prototype of a woman with a talent for philosophy' with the help of a brief selection of names and particulars from their lists of women philosophers throughout history.

A few readers may recall the names of Diotima and Aspasia: Plato introduces them in his *Symposium* and *Menexenus* respectively. In an essay about love he refers to Diotima as an authority. She is usually taken to be a fictitious character invented by Plato; but according to a critical text analysis by Waithe this is incorrect. And Aspasia, who is referred to with respect and quoted at length in Plato's *Menexenus*, is usually mentioned only as the mistress of Pericles. The fact that she was almost certainly the co-author of his famous speeches and that she must have played a leading role in the philosophical circles in which Pericles moved is generally overlooked. But at least the names of these women philosophers are still known.

Hardly anyone, however, has heard of Perictione. At school we learned that Plato was a pupil of Socrates. But why is it scarcely ever mentioned that he also owed a great deal to the wise lessons of his mother Perictione? She was a talented pupil of the school of Pythagoras, whose school

—exceptionally for the time—was also open to women. If you think of the many Pythagorean elements in Plato's work or for example the view he expressed in the *Politeia* that talented women should be able to participate in training for and practising the government of the state just like men, you realize that Plato must have received the inspiration for these ideas with his mother's milk as it were; it is very unlikely he owed them to Socrates.

While Diotima, Aspasia and Perictione all lived around the end of the fifth century BC, another woman called Hipparchia, who was just as intriguing a philosopher, lived in the late fourth century BC. She came from a good family, but against her family's wishes she gave up her comfortable life, took off her fashionable clothes and dressed in rags, joined a group of philosophers led by the cynic Crates, and became his partner. I will quote two phrases of hers from a debate with one Theodorus, as they were recorded by Diogenes Laertius in his *The Lives and Opinions of Eminent Philosophers* from later Greek antiquity (VI, 96); in contrast to Calypso's indignant outburst about the double standard, Hipparchia criticized it very calmly:

> If Theodorus would not be blamed for doing something, Hipparchia should not be blamed for doing that same thing.

And when he asked if she was the woman who had abandoned her loom, she replied:

> Yes, Theodorus, I am that person, but surely you do not think I have made the wrong decision in devoting to education that time which otherwise I should have wasted at the loom?

The context makes it quite clear that by 'education' she meant training in philosophy.

Hipparchia lived around the same time as Aristotle, one of the greatest authorities in philosophy. Aristotle based his ideas on the fundamental inequality of human beings; he believed that due to naturally inherent properties all men were superior to all women, and that certain men were superior to certain other men. He regarded all slaves as inferior but drew a distinction between those who had become slaves through circumstance, through being prisoners of war for example, and those who were slaves by nature; these he regarded as the lowliest type of human being, referring to them as *to andrapodon,* 'the human-footed creature'. Considering that Hipparchia, barefoot and clothed in rags, put herself in the position of these most despised of human beings and demonstratively proclaimed the view that all human beings were fundamentally equal, you might think that an honourable mention of her name and her opinions might have made it into the philosophy books.

The last female representative of classical thought who cannot be omitted here is Hypatia. She was a famous scholar and teacher of mathematics, astronomy, chemistry and philosophy at the Neo-Platonic School in Alexandria at around the same time that Augustine was preaching his Christian message some distance to the west on the north coast of Africa. Hypatia was loved by many for her pleasant personality, but Cyril, bishop of Alexandria, ordered this woman — in his view a dangerous heathen — to be killed. The monks who eagerly carried out his orders dragged her into a church, tore her clothes off, scraped the skin and flesh from her body with sharp shells, quartered her and finally burned her, along with most of the books she had written. This took place in 415 AD. Cyril was later canonized, whereas Hypatia was all but forgotten. Now an American journal of philosophy is named after her: *Hypatia: A Journal of Feminist Philosophy.*

The line of women philosophers certainly does not end with classical antiquity. There are two names from the Middle Ages which cannot remain unmentioned. The first is Hildegard of Bingen, a nun, composer, scientist and philosopher from the twelfth century. She wrote hundreds of letters to various church and secular rulers about all sorts of social problems. She was also the author of the book *Scivias*, a title derived from the contraction of the Latin words *scite vias*: know the ways. This work contains descriptions, illustrated by the author herself with exquisite miniatures, of her visionary experiences of Christianity. It is really these miniatures that tell us everything: they are gems, and such a breath of fresh air in comparison with Augustine's texts condemning sexuality. Whereas Augustine banished sexual pleasure to the domain of sin, Hildegard integrates it into her cosmological visions and gives it a heavenly dimension.

Another woman who made a remarkable contribution to philosophy, about two hundred years later, was Christine de Pisan. Her book *Le Livre de la Cité des Dames* (The Book of the City of Ladies), published shortly after 1400, is a superb response to the one-sided, male perspective of Augustine's *De Civitate Dei*, a work in which he depicts the creation, development and completion of the 'City of God', as it had been shaped throughout history and would continue to be shaped by many wise and gifted men. In De Pisan's book about the 'City of Ladies' — which is only one work from a sizeable oeuvre — she gives an alternative view of history, presenting dozens of names and works by wise and gifted women, in an attempt to counter the stereotyped views about them and to claim a place for talented women in the church, scholarship and society. In 1400! Certainly, there is plenty of room for criticism of her work, which does not exactly meet our standards of historical accuracy — but like Augustine, she was more concerned with presenting an allegorical sketch of an ideal society than with historical accuracy. It is a pity that for so long her antithetical reaction to Augustine's famous *De Civitate Dei* received so little attention. De Pisan's work might have played a more significant role in shaping thought about a society with balanced relationships between men and women.

Many names of women philosophers are to be found in more recent history. Over and over again, these women were faced with the task of criticizing commonly accepted views and double standards. Take for example Olympe de Gouges from the French Revolution (we will learn more about her later), or her English contemporary Mary Wollstonecraft, or from a much more recent era Harriet and Helen Taylor, whose ideas have been included in some philosophy books only under the name of John Stuart Mill. With great commitment they thought about all sorts of social injustice and strived towards fundamental equality for all human beings. The names of these women and so many other women philosophers are missing in practically all philosophy textbooks.

But surely the middle of the last century marked a definitive turning-point in this situation? From that point onwards it is impossible to imagine philosophy without women. In 1947 Simone de Beauvoir's *Pour une morale de l'ambiguïté* (The Ethics of Ambiguity) was published, and in 1949 her voluminous and famous work *Le deuxième sexe* (The Second Sex). Then in 1951 Hannah Arendt's *On the Origins of Totalitarianism* appeared, followed in 1958 by *The Human Condition*. All of these are salient philosophical works which no textbook can ignore, you might think.

However, the strange thing is that even in a recent edition of Hans Joachim Störig's popular history of philosophy De Beauvoir is not mentioned and Arendt is referred to only as a political scientist and a student of Heidegger's.

But surely an author who discusses Jean-Paul Sartre cannot fail to mention Simone de Beauvoir? In Paris in the middle of the last century they were a famous couple — the intellectual focal point of the city. The message they proclaimed was the freedom of existentialism.

In Sartre's work this freedom means a fundamental loneliness: he sees consciousness as the distinguishing feature of being human, with the consciousness of the subject perceiving the other as 'something' — an object. From Sartre's point of view there is no encounter. In her *Ethics of Ambiguity* De Beauvoir sees the distinguishing feature of being human as the unity of body and consciousness; through physical and mental emotional experience we can encounter real fellow human beings without making them into objects. In her view freedom consists of the choice each individual can make to accept emotion and connection and to determine his or her own balance of freedom and bondage.

While Sartre and De Beauvoir's joint message of existentialism was about freedom of the individual — a freedom which they thought should be attainable by all human beings — the content of their works was different. Their watchword was: 'Existentialism is a form of humanism'; but De Beauvoir realized that for women there were almost invincible barriers to freedom, that men were the first and dominant sex — the subject — whereas women had been made the object — always 'the other', the second sex. In her book *The Second Sex* dating from 1949, in over 800 pages she gives an analysis of the position of women from the perspective of cultural history. A study of such size and depth about this half of the human race was unprecedented in Western civilization. Therefore it is strange — to say the least — that Störig discusses Sartre but devotes not a single word to De Beauvoir, as though the message of freedom and the slogan 'existentialism is a form of humanism' came only from men and was important only to men.

The fact that Störig only refers to Arendt in passing as a political scientist and a student of Heidegger, without mentioning her philosophical oeuvre, is quite remarkable. It is precisely the capacity of human beings to judge that is an important theme in Arendt's oeuvre. One essay of hers which is particularly striking was written in 1963 in response to the trial of Eichmann, which she attended: *Eichmann in Jerusalem. A Report on the Banality of Evil*. The element of this trial which shocked her most was the ordinariness, the banality, of the man who was being tried: a perfectly commonplace, decent citizen, who had adopted the judgments of those in authority and obeyed their orders — with millions of deaths as a result. Respectable, everyday behaviour as the cause of evil on a large scale. This book by Hannah Arendt is a striking appeal to all of us to constantly hone our capacity to judge.

Slowly but surely it is becoming impossible to deny the conclusion that academic philosophy is a male monopoly which applies a double standard. The human being is a man — a woman is the other. And what about women philosophers? The very combination of words actually seems to contradict the objective of philosophy, since of course in principle the sex of a philosopher has nothing to do with universal insights. But because in practice one-sided judgments from the male perspective have prevailed throughout two and a half thousand years of philosophical history, it is not a bad idea to reassess the criteria according to which those women philosophers were judged and excluded. It turns out that these judgments are not as universal and non-sexist as male philosophers have often claimed.

Equal rights

While in the history of philosophy it often turns out that words like 'mankind' and 'human beings' actually referred only to 'men', and that as a result of this perspective women were excluded from philosophical discourse, political history presents even more harrowing examples of double standards. If there is one single period in history in which the misunderstanding about the concept of 'mankind' led to gruesome scenes it has to be the French Revolution. When it broke out in Paris in 1789, women fought and died side by side with men for what they believed was a shared ideal of freedom, equality and fraternity, as formulated in the famous *Déclaration des droits de l'homme et du citoyen* (Declaration of the Rights of Man and the Citizen). But it soon became clear that these 'rights of man' were certainly not intended for women as well. Women were excluded.

In 1791 the philosopher Olympe de Gouges published her *Déclaration des droits de la femme et de la citoyenne* (Declaration of the Rights of Women and the Female Citizen). A year later she organized a demonstration of women to draw attention to their struggle for equality. This struggle was to lead to her death: on 2 November 1793, in the 'Hall of Equality' — how ironic — she was condemned to the guillotine. The sentence was carried out the next day.

However, Olympe de Gouges was also sentenced to another fate. While history books always devote a great deal of attention to the French Revolution and refer to many of the male protagonists, the name of Olympe de Gouges is very rarely mentioned. She has been ignored — treated as an insignificant player in a struggle for human rights which turned out to be actually only a struggle for the rights of men. The memory of this militant advocate of human rights for *all* human beings has almost faded away;

she has become one of the many forgotten minor figures in the history of Western civilization.

It was not until 1948 that the basic equality of all human beings was laid down in the *Universal Declaration of the Rights of Man* and later defined in more detail in various UN treaties. Human rights for women were laid down in 1979 in a UN treaty with the somewhat laborious title *Convention on the Elimination of all Forms of Discrimination against Women* — usually referred to as CEDAW. By now this treaty has been ratified by most UN member states. The Netherlands was not one of the first; it only ratified the treaty in 1991. The United States has still not done so.

Of course these UN treaties in which the principle of equality for all human beings is laid down in detail do not provide any guarantee whatsoever that the principle will be observed in practice. Views and practices which have been taken for granted for centuries are inclined to be tenacious. But the declaration of basic principles itself is certainly a milestone in the history of civilization.

Women in academic philosophy today

At present a true revolution is taking place in the academic world; that world is no longer the exclusive domain of men. Today the numerical relationship of male and female students is about fifty-fifty. Now that women — and therefore different perspectives — have entered the academic realm, should academic insights also be adapted? Departments of Women's Studies have been set up in all the faculties to examine these questions. However, because this book focuses mainly on classical texts with philosophical implications, so that value judgments with respect to these texts have been formed mainly in the field of philosophy, at this point I will briefly discuss developments in women's studies in philosophy.

There are three main fields of activity in this area. The first covers questions about women philosophers throughout history and what their ideas were; as we saw earlier in this chapter there were many of these, but they have been almost entirely forgotten. About six centuries after Christine de Pisan's death, the threads of her work had to be picked up again; a new history of women philosophers needed to be written, which met present-day academic criteria and included many new names and works. Earlier, we already mentioned Mary Warren's encyclopedia, *The Nature of Woman*, published in 1980 and the four part *History of Women Philosophers* by Mary Ellen Waithe, published between 1989 and 1995. But we must not fail to mention the *Encyclopedia of Feminist Theories,* published in 2003, edited by Lorraine Code. Another book — less bulky but very readable — is *Dialogues on Women* by Louise Derksen of the Philosophy Department of the VU University, Amsterdam, published in 1996. At present, the topic women and philosophy is a subject of research in many countries and languages. There are journals, such as *Hypatia. A Journal of Feminist Philosophy*, and international associations such as the originally German Internationale Assoziation von Philosophinnen/International Association of Women Philosophers which try to promote the philosophical thinking of women throughout the world.

A second field of activities is research into the blind spots of male philosophers as a result of their one-sided perspective. For example, the Norwegian philosopher Vigdis Songe-Møller recently published an excellent study entitled *Philosophy Without Women. The Birth of Sexism in Western Thought*. Many examples of this phenomenon, throughout all periods of history, can in fact be traced back to the origins of sexism as she describes them. And anyone who thinks that Immanuel Kant, who always formulated his ideas with extreme care, never made any blunders, should read the penetrating analyses written by the American philosopher Nancy Tuana and the Dutch philosopher Paulien Kleingeld in *Against Patriarchal Thinking*, a volume of the proceedings of a conference of women philosophers (Amsterdam 1992, Pellikaan-Engel (ed.)). Tuana points out in her paper that although Kant postulates that human beings may never use others simply as a means to something else, but must always see them as an end in themselves — and that the development of man's rational capacities is essential to the formation of a moral character — he nevertheless considers that this kind of development is not suited to women: it would only upset the development of men. Therefore in his view women are merely a means for something else, namely the perfection of men's development. Kleingeld also shows that while Kant quite often uses terms which seem to have a generic meaning, such as 'everyone', 'man', 'mankind', it becomes evident that women are not included in these concepts. Apparently Kant himself violates his own moral principle that you should always 'act as if the maxim from which you act were to become through your will a universal law'. In many cases the 'universal' laws he postulates in his theories are not universal, but sex-specific.

A third field of activities in women's studies in philosophy is the participation of women in current philosophical debate. Sometimes people ask what the specifically female contribution is to philosophical discourse, which until the present time has been general. Anyone who has followed the reasoning of this book will realize that this is an incorrect question, in two respects. Firstly, until the present day there has never been a 'general' philosophical discourse; those taking part in the discussion were usually all members of a small group of — in most cases white — men. Secondly, it is impossible to talk about a 'specifically female contribution'; this kind of traditional stereotype is incorrect in itself. In practice it turns out that if women take part in the discourse, they often simply connect with commonly accepted views; moreover, they rarely agree with each other entirely — and sometimes they totally disagree. But the enrichment of philosophy through the participation of women lies mainly in the additional perspectives it offers; women, just like men, can all examine the existing topics from different, individual angles, with different, individual approaches, and will therefore sometimes also raise different problems and questions.

For example, I myself asked the question in what circumstances it is justifiable to bring new people into the world. Until recently this was an extremely unusual question in philosophy; it is a question Socrates might well have asked himself, and in view of present developments in medical technology such as sperm, egg and embryo donation it now reflects an urgent problem in society. In my opinion this problem should be approached with careful consideration of the human rights of all those involved, including the rights of the future children — such as the right to know and be cared for by their own parents, as set out in the Convention on the Rights of the Child — so that the principle stated in Article 1 of the Universal Declaration of Human Rights that all human beings are 'born equal in dignity and rights' also truly applies to them.

The developments in women's studies make it increasingly clear that the imbalance in academic practice is due not only to the physical absence of women in academia, but also to the gender stereotypes on which that absence was based. Gender stereotypes are personality features attributed to men and women in a society purely on the basis of their sex. For example, rationality has come to be thought of as a typically male characteristic, whereas emotionality is associated with women. Everything thought of as being masculine has a higher prestige and is far removed from everything deemed to be feminine — and lo and behold, we have an unbridgeable gap between reason and emotion, and between *apatheia* and empathy. Of course this is not really true, since emotions and intellect are present in every human being as different aspects of consciousness, and ideally an individual attempts to find a balance between the two, but the effects of this gender stereotype in social reality are very persistent. At present there is a tendency in women's studies to focus mainly on these socially determined identities which are attributed to the sexes and the consequences they have for society. Women's studies is becoming more and more the domain of gender studies.

An important area within gender studies is gender linguistics. Anyone who has followed my analyses in the previous chapters should not be put off by this term: all of my critical text analyses can actually be termed 'gender analyses' and classified as gender linguistics. The point is that asymmetrical relationships in society not only manifest themselves in language but are also preserved by language. Gender linguistics studies the ways in which language pins people down to the identities which have been imposed on them and the possibilities offered by language to break away from thought patterns of this kind.

In the Netherlands Agnes Verbiest, lecturer in gender linguistics at Leiden University, has published several books on this topic in which she shows—often in an amusing way—how much we take these asymmetrical thought patterns for granted. A quotation from a recent publication by Agnes Verbiest and her colleague Agnes Sneller may serve as an illustration of the gender content of the thinking of some philosophers. This quotation is taken from a New Year's gift for 2000 sent by the International School of Philosophy in Leusden to its associates. It included a philosophical essay—intended to be universal—about love by the Dutch philosopher Frans Jacobs. Alluding to a passage about love in American philosopher Robert Nozick's prestigious book *Anarchy, State and Utopia* he says:

> You love someone, because of her beautiful eyes, her graceful figure and because she spoils you.

Sneller and Verbiest's comment:

> The generic 'you' turns out to be specifically male. The gender content created by the one-sided male use of the indefinite 'you' not only excludes women, but also creates a 'man to man' atmosphere which is taken for granted.

That one little word 'you' — it is no more than a molecule of our everyday language. But in this context it is also a molecule of injustice against women, because it is an affirmation of the asymmetrical image of humanity in philosophy: mankind is a man, a woman is the other.

Rationality

The integration of women into academic philosophy is a laborious process. There are plenty of women students, but if you look at the number of women lecturers it is difficult to avoid comparisons with certain relationships in the church; the further you go up the ladder, the fewer women there are, even more so than in most other faculties. The current professors would indubitably assert that their judgments are always based on purely rational grounds and that the simple fact is that academic philosophy is a purely rational business.

It has become quite clear that in reality double standards have been applied all too often throughout the history of philosophy. It is far from certain whether rationality according to the currently prevailing view will suffice to identify and eliminate blind spots in philosophy with respect to sex and gender. Many philosophers think that this process is simply a question of making some corrections on rational grounds. The American philosopher Martha Nussbaum, for example, is confident that men will be quite prepared to enter into rational discussions with women in order to change both their insights and the present situation at universities. Louise Derksen, a philosopher from Amsterdam, is less optimistic. In her critical analysis of Nussbaum, Derksen says that women's studies will have to bring about a revolutionary change which will involve overturning the perception of rationality in the academic world itself.

However, this discussion falls outside the scope of this book. For the concept of rationality in philosophy, let us return to the very beginning of the history of philosophy. The word philosophy, coined by Pythagoras in about 500 BC, means 'love of wisdom'. The maxim inscribed on the temple of Delphi was regarded as the basis of wisdom: 'Know thyself' — an appeal to self-reflection, a call to find out more about your own identity, character, capacities, emotions and motivations with the help of your reason. In the preceding chapters we have seen that not only were there blind spots in the self-reflection of several highly-praised philosophers, but that these blind spots were often not recognized by later philosophers or regarded as unimportant.

The crucial role originally attributed to self-reflection has disappeared into the background. The concept of rationality which now plays the leading role in academic philosophy has different implications and as such has a lot in common with Seneca's *apatheia*: it is rationality as opposed to emotionality. It does not aspire to understand emotions and motivations with the help of reason, but to repress them and to leave any further study of them to psychologists. The rationality of *apatheia* excludes the understanding of emotions and empathy. This meagre concept of rationality seems to be the defining feature of the stereotype of male philosophers, whereas emotionality — usually taken to mean *hyper*-sensibility or imbalance — is the pivotal feature of the stereotype of women. Because of this women have been almost automatically disqualified for philosophy, which after all is regarded as a purely rational discipline.

However, fortunately this section does not have to end in a minor key. There really are signs of a revolution in this world of stereotyped thinking. Not only are more and more women managing to penetrate into the world of academic philosophy, but the monoculture of rationality which has been predominant there is being challenged and more attention is being paid to the positive value of emotions. On this score Nussbaum's *Upheavals of Thought: The Intelligence of Emotions* (2001) marks a turning-point in philosophical thought. In this superb book she uses a large number of texts from philosophy and literature throughout history to illustrate that emotions actually imply value judgments and makes a strong case for using our feelings of empathy and compassion as a basis for morally responsible citizenship.

Calypso's moral principle

Via this plea for empathy and compassion I will now return to the oldest literary work of Western civilization — Homer's Odyssey, with Calypso's oath as a moral guideline. How did she put it again?

> But I am only thinking of and shall ponder on what
> I should devise for myself, if I were in your straits;
> for my mind is righteous and the heart in this breast
> of mine is not of iron, but has compassion.
> (*Od.* 5.188-91, tr. M. Pellikaan-Engel.)

We have seen that with this very personal statement she was actually formulating a well-considered moral principle, which drew on empathy as the force driving reason and intellect to focus on finding solutions for problems which are making people's lives difficult. But this was not all. She also showed great commitment to putting this theory into practice; with her own hands she helped Odysseus to build and stock the ship which was to reunite him with Penelope after so many years. Then the man she loved sailed away. Homer has depicted her as a character of tremendous moral strength, who combines empathy, rationality and practical commitment. In Calypso the poet has given us a model of philosophical wisdom which academic philosophers should not simply ignore. With an attitude based on precisely these three components they should be able to bridge not only the gap between theory and practice, but also that between men and women in philosophy.

For today there are still two worlds. On the one hand there is the self-enclosed world of academic philosophy, which is the domain of intellectuals who focus their attention mainly on libraries full of publications on theories about abstract concepts such as 'mankind' and 'justice'. This world closely resembles the proverbial ivory tower, where men play most of the leading roles, but from which they also exert influence and authority and sometimes even leave their mark on moral judgments which affect the whole community. An imbalance in their views is therefore certainly not irrelevant: younger generations learn to see through their eyes and thus inherit the blind spots in their judgments about the other world — the 'ordinary' world of people who take care of other people who are dependent on help: small children, the sick, the disabled, the old and the dying. This is a world in which women are usually amply represented.

These two worlds—the theory of academic philosophy and the reality of everyday care—are usually separated from each other. And what that other world actually means — the expectations another individual has of you, the appeal to your capacity for empathy and concrete help, the impact of these things on your views on concepts like 'mankind' and 'justice' — seldom penetrates into the abstract, intellectual world of philosophers. All too often they have deemed themselves to be exemplary models for 'mankind' without truly knowing themselves and their fellow human beings. But those who actually care for children, or the sick, elderly or dying — phases we have all gone through or will go through in the future — learn to know themselves through the other and the other through themselves — just as in a love relationship perception of oneself and empathy with the other increase through the reciprocal exchange of intimacy.

But if we want to make empathy an essential component of philosophy we cannot ignore practical reality. What empathy means cannot be learned through books and theory — and certainly not *only* through books and theory. Experience of the everyday reality of contact and care for others is essential. All those who wish to engage in academic philosophy professionally should therefore be required to be practically involved in caring for other human beings, at least part-time.

A measure like this might prove to be an efficacious remedy for the blind spots which crop up again and again in philosophy with respect to the abstract concept of 'man', which philosophers have so often given a meaning based on their own perceptions and those of their (white, male) fellow philosophers. But there is no such thing as 'man'. The addition of a different perspective, through practical involvement in caring for even a few fellow human beings, could be an eye-opener, leading to greater insight, both into the wide diversity of our countless fellow human beings and into our own identity. Although it may be impossible to avoid blind spots altogether, better insight into one's own identity and that of the other might lead to better understanding and more balanced relationships; and who knows, it might even put an end to the age-old segregation between men and women in philosophy.

Another consequence of compulsory practical involvement with real fellow human beings would probably be a greater involvement of philosophers in the fundamental and practical consequences of modern technological developments today and in the future. We have now arrived in the twenty-first century. Technology has already run away with humanity to a certain extent. But too often academic philosophers still try to emulate Seneca's *apatheia*. It is about time philosophers — both men and women — got rid of this model of rationality and took the moral principle formulated by Homer's Calypso as a guideline, so that through a combination of empathy, rationality and practical involvement they can search for solutions to the problems of humanity — because we hold it dear.

Sources

The list below does not include references to the specific editions of Greek and Latin texts discussed in the book. All of these texts are to be found in the Loeb Classical Library published by William Heinemann LTD, London and Harvard University Press in Cambridge, MA. This collection shows the Greek or Latin texts with English translations on the opposite pages. However, unless otherwise specified the translations of the quotations in this book are by Margaret Kofod.

2 *Calypso*

HOMER, *Iliad; Odyssee.*
KUNDERA, M., *Ignorance*, translated by Linda Asher. Faber, 2001.
Novum Testamentum Graece (see under Sources 6, St Augustine).
POMEROY, SARAH B., *Goddesses, Whores, Wives, and Slaves: Women in Classical Antiquity.* New York: Schocken Books, 1975.
VIRGIL, *Aeneid.*

3 *Socrates and Xanthippe*

ARISTOPHANES, *Nubes.*
BURY, J. B., *A History of Greece.* London: Macmillan, New York: St Martin's Press, 3rd edition 1959.
HUPPERTS, C., JANS, E., STORK, P., BOOT, P., *Plato. Een weg naar de waarheid* [Plato: a Way to the Truth]. Leeuwarden: Eisma BV, 1992.
PLATO, *Apology; Crito; Phaedo.*
STONE, I. F., *The Trial of Socrates.* Random House, 1988.
XENOPHON, *Memorabilia; Symposium.*

SOURCES

4 *Cicero*

CARY, M., *A History of Rome*. London: Macmillan. New York: St. Martin's Press, 2nd edition 1957.

CICERO, *Epistulae ad Atticum; Epistulae ad Familiares; De Re Publica*.

ENK, DR P. J., *Geschiedenis der Latijnse Letterkunde* [History of Latin Literature]. Groningen, Jakarta: J.B. Wolters, 4th impression 1956.

KASSIES, W., *Cicero. Brieven* [Cicero: Letters]. Bussum: Fibula-Van Dishoeck, 1972.

KASSIES, W., 'Tullia, Cicero's dochter' [Tullia, Cicero's daughter] in *Hermeneus, Tijdschrift voor Antieke Cultuur* [Hermeneus, Journal of Antiquity] vol. 69, no. 3. Alkmaar: Ter Burg Offset, 1997.

KUNNEMAN, H., *Postmoderne Moraliteit* [Postmodern Morality]. Amsterdam: Boom, 1998.

PLATO, *Politeia*.

5 *Seneca*

NUSSBAUM, M., *The Therapy of Desire: Theory and Practice in Hellenistic Ethics*. Princeton: Princeton University Press, 1994.

SCHRIJVERS, P. H., 'Het voortleven van de omstreden Seneca' ['Ongoing controversy on Seneca'] in *Seneca Sapiens, Negen Epistulae morales in filosofische en cultuurhistorische context* [Seneca Sapiens, Nine Epistulae Morales in their Philosophical and Cultural-Historical Context], Goris, M., Fisser, C., Rijke, P., Verhoeven, P., Vester, E. 's Hertogenbosch: Malmberg, 1991.

SENECA, *Epistulae ad Lucilium; Medea*.

SENECA, *Brieven aan Lucilius* [Letters to Lucilius], translated into Dutch by Cornelis Verhoeven, with an introduction and notes. Baarn: Uitgeverij Ambo, 1980.

TACITUS, *Annals*.

6 Augustine

AUGUSTINE, *Confessiones; De Civitate Dei; Soliloquia.*
CARROLL, JAMES, 'From celibacy to godliness' in the *Boston Globe* (04.09.2004).
NESTLE, E., *Novum Testamentum Graece.* Stuttgart: Privilegierte Würtembergische Bibelanstalt, 1936.
REMARK, PETER, *Augustinus Selbstgespräche. S. Aurelii Augustini Soliloquiorum libri duo.* Munich: Heimeran, 1965.
WILLS, GARRY, *Saint Augustine.* New York: Viking Penguin, 1999.

8 Women and the history of philosophy

ARENDT, HANNAH, *The Origins of Totalitarianism.* New York: Harcourt Brace, 1951.
ARENDT, HANNAH, *The Human Condition.* Chicago: University of Chicago Press, 1958.
ARENDT, HANNAH, *Eichmann in Jerusalem. A report on the banality of evil.* 1st impression 1963. New York: Viking Press, 1970.
ARISTOTLE, *De Generatione Animalium, Ethica Nicomachea, Politica.*
BEAUVOIR, SIMONE DE, *The Second Sex*, translated from the French by H. M. Parshley. Penguin 1972.
BEAUVOIR, SIMONE DE, *The Ethics of Ambiguity*, translated from the French by Bernard Frechtman. Secaucus NJ: Citadel Press, 1949.
BINGEN, HILDEGARD OF, *Scivias.* With comments on the miniatures (in Dutch), by Brother Henri Boelaars O.S.B. Katwijk aan Zee: Servire Uitgevers B.V., 1984.
CODE, LORRAINE, ed., *Encyclopedia of Feminist Theories.* London, Routledge, 2003.
DERKSEN, L. D., *Dialogues on Women. Images of Women in the History of Philosophy.* http://hdl.handle.net/1871/12766 165 p. This is the electronic publication of the book which was published in Amsterdam VU University Press, 1996.
DERKSEN, LOUISE, 'Martha Nussbaum on Rationality, Tolerance and Liberation. How Rational Should Women's Studies Be?' in Birgit Christensen (ed.) *wissen macht geschlecht / knowledge power gender.* Zürich: Chronos Verlag, 2002, pp. 439-446.
DIOGENES LAERTIUS, *De clarorum philosophorum vitis.*

SOURCES

DIOGENES LAERTIUS, *Leven en leer van beroemde filosofen* [Lives and Teachings of Famous Philosophers], translated into Dutch by Dr Rein Ferwerda and Dr Jan Eykman. Baarn: Uitgeverij Ambo, 1989.

GAARDER, JOSTEIN, *Sophie's World: A Novel about the History of Philosophy*, translated from Norwegian by Paulette Møller. London: Phoenix, 1995.

GOUGES, OLYMPE DE, *Verklaring van de rechten van de vrouw en burgeres*, translation from French into Dutch by Anja Hélène of *Déclaration des Droits de la Femme et de la Citoyenne* [Declaration of the Rights of Woman and the Female Citizen] (Paris 1791), with an introduction and commentary by Hannelore Schröder. Kampen: Kok Agora, 1989.

Hypatia. A Journal of Feminist Philosophy. 1986-present. Bloomington, Indiana, Indiana University Press.

JASPERS, KARL, *Die grossen Philosophen I* [The Great Philosophers I]. Munich: R. Piper & Co Verlag, 1959.

KLEINGELD, PAULIEN, 'When "He or She" Won't Do', in Pellikaan-Engel, M.E. (ed.), *Against Patriarchal Thinking. A Future Without discrimination?* Amsterdam: VU University Press, 1992.

MILL, JOHN STUART, *De onderwerping van de vrouw*. Dutch translation by Eva Wolff of *The Subjection of Women* (1869), with an introduction by Maaike Meijer. Meppel: Boom, 1981.

NUSSBAUM, MARTHA, *Upheavals of Thought: The Intelligence of Emotions*. Cambridge University Press, 2001.

NOZICK, ROBERT, *Anarchy, State, and Utopia*. Oxford: Blackwell, 1974.

PELLIKAAN-ENGEL, MAJA, 'Feminism and Justice: Not without Children's Rights', in Christensen, Birgit (ed.), *wissen macht geschlecht / knowledge power gender*. Zürich: Chronos Verlag, 2002.

PISAN, CHRISTINE DE, *Het Boek van de Stad der Vrouwen*, translated from French into Dutch by Tine Pontfoort of *Livre de la Cité des Dames* (Paris 1405) with an introduction by the translator. Amsterdam: Feministische Uitgeverij Sara, 1984.

PLATO, *Apology; Menexenus; Politeia; Symposium.*

SNELLER, A. AGNES & VERBIEST, AGNES, *Bij wijze van schrijven. Over gender en trefzeker taalgebruik* [In a Manner of Writing: on Gender and Accurate Use of Language]. The Hague: Sdu Uitgevers, 2002.

SONGE-MØLLER, VIGDIS, *Philosophy Without Women. The Birth of Sexism in Western Thought*. London, New York: Continuum, 2002.

STÖRIG, HANS JOACHIM, *Geschiedenis van de filosofie*. Translated from German into Dutch (original title *Kleine Weltgeschichte der Philosophie*) by Brommer, Dr P., Brink, J. K. van den, et al., 1959. Utrecht: Het Spectrum 26th impression, 2002.

TUANA, NANCY, 'Reading Philosophy as a Woman', in Maja Pellikaan-Engel (ed.), *Against Patriarchal Thinking. A Future Without Discrimination?* Amsterdam: VU University Press, 1992.

WAITHE, MARY ELLEN, (ed.), *A History of Women Philosophers Vol. I, 600 BC–500 AD*; *Vol. II: Medieval, Renaissance and Enlightenment Women Philosophers, 500–1600*; *Vol. III: Modern Women Philosophers, 1600–1900*; *Vol. IV: Contemporary Women Philosophers, 1900–today*. Dordrecht/Boston/London: previously Martinus Nijhoff Publishers, now Kluwer Academic Publishers, 1987–1995.

WARREN, MARY ANNE, *The Nature of Woman. An Encyclopedia and Guide to the Literature*. Inverness, California, Edgepress, 1980.

WINDELBAND, WILHELM, Heimsoeth, Heinz, *Lehrbuch der Geschichte der Philosophie*. Tübingen: J.C.B. Mohr (Paul Siebeck), 15th impression 1957.

Index

Adeodatus 68, 72, 73
Aemilius Paullus 46, 48
Aeneas 26
Alcibiades 34, 35
Antisthenes 29
Aphrodite 25
Arendt, H. 90, 92, 109
Aristophanes 32, 107
Aristotle 88, 109
Artemis 15
Asclepius 42
Aspasia 86, 87
Athena 18, 19, 25
Atlas 18, 19
Atticus 51, 53
Augustine 10-12, 54, 66-76, 79, 88-90, 109
Augustus 55, 68

Beauvoir, S. de 90, 91, 109
Berlioz, H. 26
Bingen, H. of 89, 109
Buddha 43
Bury, J.B. 107

Calypso 9-11, 14-18, 20, 22-27, 30, 32, 77, 84, 86, 101, 102, 104
Carroll, J. 66, 76, 109
Cary, M. 108
Cicero 10-12, 44-55, 67, 68, 74, 78, 79, 81, 82, 108
Circe 20
Code, L. 95, 109
Confucius 83

Crates 87
Crito 38, 40-42
Cyril 88

Dawn 15
Demeter 15
Derksen, L. 95, 100, 109
Dido 26
Diogenes Laërtius 87, 109, 110
Diotima 84, 86, 87
Dolabella 52

Eichmann, A. 92
Enk, P.J. 81, 108
Euripides 63

Gaarder, J. 84, 85, 110
Gouges, O. de 90, 93, 110
Gracchus, G. and Tib. 47, 48

Heidegger, M. 90, 92
Helen 20
Hera 25
Hermes 15
Hipparchia 87, 88
Homer 11, 15, 18-27, 77, 101, 102, 104, 107
Hupperts, C. a.o. 107
Hypatia 88, 110

Jacobs, F. 98
Jasion 15
Jason 63
Jaspers, K. 41, 43, 83, 84, 110
Jesus 43, 83

INDEX

Juno 25
Jupiter 57

Kant, I. 24, 25, 29, 95, 96
Kassies, W. 50, 108
Kleingeld, P. 96, 110
Kundera, M. 26, 107
Kunneman, H. 44, 108

Lentulus 52

Mani 67
Marcellinus 61
Marcus 50
Medea 63
Mill, J.S. 90, 110
Minerva 25
Monica 12, 66-70, 72, 73, 75, 76

Nero 10, 55, 56, 60
Nozick, R. 98, 110
Nussbaum, M. 63, 100, 101, 108, 110

Odysseus 15-23, 25, 26, 77, 102
Orion 15

Patricius 66, 67
Paulina 56-60, 64, 79
Pellikaan-Engel, M. 96, 110
Penelope 9, 15, 19-22, 26, 27, 102
Pericles 86
Perictione 86, 87
Phaedo 40, 41
Pisan, C. de 89, 90, 95, 110
Plato 9, 10, 28, 32, 35, 36, 38-43, 45, 56, 67, 71, 86, 87, 107, 108, 110
Pomeroy, S. B. 25, 107
Purcell, H. 26

Publilia 52
Pythagoras 86, 100

Sartre, J. P. 91
Schrijvers, P. 65, 108
Scipio Aem. 10, 45-47, 49, 51, 53, 78, 81
Scipio Maior 46
Seneca 10-12, 55-65, 79, 100, 104, 108
Sneller, A. A. 98, 99, 110
Socrates 9-12, 28-43, 56-59, 77-79, 82, 84-87, 97
Songe-Møller, V. 95, 110
Stone, I.F. 34, 107
Störig, H. J. 84, 90-92, 111

Tacitus 10, 56, 57, 60, 108
Taylor, H. 90
Taylor Mill, H. 90
Terentia 50-52
Theodoros 87
Tuana, N. 96, 111
Tullia 12, 50-52, 78

Una 75

Venus 25
Verbiest, A. 98, 99, 110
Virgil 26, 67, 72, 107

Waithe, M. E. 86, 95, 111
Warren, M. A. 86, 95, 111
Wills, G. 66, 67, 69, 71, 75, 109
Windelband, W. 82-84, 111
Wollstonecraft, M. 90

Xanthippe 9, 10, 28-33, 37, 40-43, 58, 78, 79, 82-84
Xenophon 9, 28-30, 107

Zeus 15, 17, 18

ACKNOWLEDGMENTS

I would like to thank Dr Jan Maarten Bremer, emeritus professor of classical Greek literature at the University of Amsterdam, Dr Loes Derksen, philosophy lecturer in Women's Studies at the VU University of Amsterdam, Caroline Fisser, lecturer in classics teaching methods at the VU University of Amsterdam, Dr Marietje d'Hane-Scheltema, former classics lecturer and translator of Greek and Latin poetry, Professor Irene de Jong, professor of classical Greek literature at the University of Amsterdam, John Nagelkerken, former colleague at Murmellius Gymnasium in Alkmaar, Dr Agnes Verbiest, former lecturer in Dutch speech communication and gender linguistics at Leiden University and Dr Mariëtte Willemsen, lecturer in modern philosophy at the VU University of Amsterdam. I am very grateful to all of them for their valuable comments on my manuscript. Above all I would like to say that without the encouragement and moral support of Agnes Verbiest this book would not have been written. I am very grateful to the staff of the Taalcentrum VU in Amsterdam for the English translation. I would particularly like to thank Margaret Kofod for translating this book with such skill and commitment.

ABOUT THE AUTHOR

Dr Maja Pellikaan-Engel (1937) worked as a classics teacher at Murmellius Gymnasium in Alkmaar. She is married and has children and grandchildren. Dr Pellikaan-Engel obtained her doctorate in philosophy with the dissertation *Hesiod and Parmenides: A New View on their Cosmologies and on Parmenides' Proem.* Amsterdam: Adolf M. Hakkert, 1974, 1978.

She is a former board member of the IAPh: Internationale Assoziation von Philosophinnen/International Association of Women Philosophers (www.iaph-philo.org) and was the editor of *Against Patriarchal Thinking: A Future without Discrimination?* Amsterdam: VU University Press, 1992.

Dr Pellikaan-Engel has given lectures and published articles on classical texts and on the human rights of women and children. Her lecture on Socrates during the World Congress of Philosophy in Brighton in 1988 caused quite a stir. *The Guardian* wrote about it on 27/08/88 under the heading 'Why Socrates should have heeded his missus'. Her contribution to the IAPh symposium in Zürich in 2000: 'Feminism and Justice: Not without Children's Rights' may be found in *wissen macht geschlecht / knowledge power gender*, ed. Birgit Christensen. Zürich: Chronos Verlag 2002, pp. 229-237.

In 2004 she put out *Het recept van Calypso. Klassieke teksten in een hedendaags filosofisch perspectief* (Damon Publishers, Budel), translated by Margaret Kofod and published, with minor adjustments, as *Calypso's Oath*.

http://www.pellikaanengel.nl